MINISTERS AS LEADERS

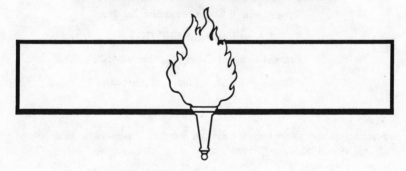

Robert D. Dale

BROADMAN PRESS
Nashville, Tennessee

© Copyright 1984 • Broadman Press

All Rights Reserved

4231-10

ISBN: 0-8054-3110-1

Dewey Decimal Classification Number: 253

Subject Headings: MINISTERS

Library of Congress Catalog Number: 84-9501

Printed in the United States of America

Scripture quotations are from the Revised Standard Version of the Bible, copyrighted 1946, 1952, © 1971, 1973.

Library of Congress Cataloging in Publication Data

Dale, Robert D.
  Ministers as leaders.

  1. Christian leadership.   I. Title.
BV652.1.D34   1984   262'.1   84-9501
ISBN 0-8054-3110-1 (pbk.)

Acknowledgments

Books tend to list only the author's name on their covers. The writers of books know that a team effort underlies the product readers finally see. I acknowledge that this book builds on the ideas and work of many people.

Thanks to the Center for Creative Leadership for providing a stimulating sabbatical setting and plentiful resources. David De-Vries, Bob Kaplan, Randy White, Frank Freeman, and Karen Barden have provided front-line assistance at the center.

Invaluable feedback on the rough draft of this book was provided by Michael G. Queen, Dennis L. Stamey, Vern Peterson, Mike H. Jamison, and Jim Jarrard.

Thanks to Don Hammer, Jere Allen, Bill Pinson, and Doran McCarty for their initiative in planning and launching the Broadman Leadership Series.

Thanks to ministers' seminars and seminary classes in which these ideas were polished. Thanks to Mrs. Mary Lou Stephens who patiently prepared the manuscript. And thanks to the late Wesley Williams who provided inspiration for this project.

72507

Contents

Foreword

Leader style has a ripple effect. As a pebble tossed into a pond sends ripples toward all shores, leader styles make waves too. After all, that's part of the purpose of leadership—to influence others to choose a purposeful direction.

"How" is often at least as crucial as "what" in leadership. For example, how a ministry leader behaves may do more to leaven a congregation than what a leader tries to influence followers to do. All of us have seen leaders attempt good things in bad ways and injure congregations in the process. Therefore, style and content are bound together in leadership.

This book explores leader styles: what they are, where they come from, and what they do to and for others. Whether leadership is practiced by pastors or laypersons, leader styles have a ripple effect in congregations.

Ripples create movement. Taken to extremes, ripples may become destructive tidal waves. In the interest of healthy churches, the ripples I propose are catalytic in style, congregational in context, fraternal in attitude, and interactive in practice.

Throughout this book I use he and other masculine pronouns in a generic sense. I recognize the role of men and women as leaders in churches.

I
Foundations for Congregational Leadership

1
Options:
A Smorgasbord of Styles

Quick! Put your thinking cap on and ask yourself five practical leader-style questions.

- Why do you try to lead?
- How do you get to lead?
- Are the results of your leader style predictable?
- Where do you place your leadership priorities?
- How does your leader style fit congregational needs?

Lots of leadership researchers have tried to answer these basic questions. Some of their findings fit churches and volunteer organizations particularly well. These discoveries provide us with a mixture of ingredients for a congregational leadership model.

Why Do You Try to Lead?

The results and motives of leaders vary widely. James Mac-Gregor Burns identifies two types of leaders. According to Burns, the transacting leader is primarily involved in exchanging one thing for another; he bargains consciously in order to trade values. The transacting leader develops *quid pro quo*—something for something—relationships. The transacting leader allocates existing resources and, at best, manages them efficiently.

On the other hand, Burns sees the real genius of leadership in the transforming leader. Transforming leaders engage their followers by intending to satisfy the followers' higher needs and motives. He suggests, "The result of transforming leadership is a relationship of mutual stimulation and elevation that converts followers into leaders and may convert leaders into moral agents."[1]

What does a transforming moral agent do? Mobilizes. Inspires. Exalts. Uplifts. Evangelizes. Exhorts. In the final analysis, transforming leadership "becomes *moral* in that it raises the level of human conduct and ethical aspiration of both leader and led, and thus has a transforming effect on both."[2] Stated in congregational terms, as the leader exercises initiative, the morale level of members is raised and ministry happens.

Transactors are custodians who maintain; transformers are motivators who build. What are you trying to do in your leader efforts? Why are you trying to lead?

How Do You Get to Lead?

Leaders don't tumble out of the sky full-blown and credible. Some legitimatizing process opens the door to leadership for us. Leaders of volunteer organizations are allowed to lead by their followers. Research has pointed toward two legitimation processes.[3]

Some leaders are appointed. That is, they are put in charge by an outside authority like a boss or a board. This kind of legitimacy is common in some denominations who appoint ministers as well as in ministry agencies and the corporate world. Appointed leaders are more typical of formal organizations.

Other leaders simply emerge. Emergent leaders secure a willing following by group election or by some less defined and formalized processes allowing prominence, visibility, and dominance to develop. This type of legitimacy is typical of unstructured work groups, athletic teams, social groups, and gangs. Emergent leadership depends heavily on the followers' interests and moods. Therefore, emergent leaders have fairly insecure status since the support of their followers can be withdrawn at any time. Most congregational leaders have emerged out of service in the church's mainstream.

Recently, I heard Herschel Hobbs comment on how a minister's work becomes accepted in a congregation. His statement describes emergent leadership. According to Hobbs, "A congregational vote makes you the preacher, worship leader, and administrator immediately. But it takes two to five years for you really to become the pastor of a church." Hobbs notes that some ministry roles can be appointed while others emerge. Another implication of Hobbs's statement is that the servant-leader model of the New Testament (Mark 10:42-45) describes primarily emergent leadership.

The character of emergent leadership changes over time, especially where pastors are concerned. A congregational vote establishes you in a role. But roles tend to erode as time passes. Remember the old saying "Familiarity breeds contempt"? Relationships must be developed and banked against the day when the role account may be drawn down to bankruptcy. A vote places the pastor in a church with a leader role; relationships keep a pastor effective within that congregation as time changes his status.

How do we get to lead? Whether we are appointed or have emerged from our group, folks let us lead. They see potential in us and hope for results through us.

Are the Results of Your Leader Style Predictable?

Who you are determines what you do as a leader. At least that's the claim of James David Barber, Duke University's political scientist. Barber thinks the personalities of American presidents can be studied to predict their performance in office. Barber notes our chief executives are either "active" or "passive" in the conduct of their office and in their relationships with their constituents. They are also, according to Barber, either "positive" or "negative" in their feelings about power and the pursuit of goals.

Barber combines these factors into patterns and categorizes our presidents accordingly. For instance, Barber sees both Roosevelts, John Kennedy, and Harry Truman as "active-positives." They were active in their relationships and comfortable with the exercise of their office. Tragedy-prone presidents like Nixon and Lyndon Johnson are placed in the "active-negative" niche. Their negative use of power was a fatal flaw according to Barber. Reagan, Harding, and Taft are "passive-positives" in Barber's system. These presidents weren't able to exercise initiative toward others easily. Finally, Barber uses Coolidge as one example of a "passive-negative" president.[4]

Are you comfortable approaching people? Or do you prefer to leave the relational initiative with others? Can you work on developing and implementing group goals? Or would you rather push your own goals in group settings? Your character will probably make your leader style predictable. After all, we act on what we value. None of us is a better leader than he is a person.

Where Do You Place Your Leadership Priorities?

Do you attend to people's needs first and allow organizational issues to slide? Or do you pursue goals in gung ho fashion even though members' toes get stepped on frequently? A nice guy or an achiever? Both? Leadership models commonly have dealt with two dimensions of behavior: task and relationships. Production or people provide double-edged tension. A common leadership topic, therefore, is how to balance these two behavioral dimensions in actual practice.

Robert Blake and Jane Mouton have developed an approach dramatizing leader's priorities.[5] Their managerial grid model is based on a vertical axis emphasizing "concern for people" and a horizontal axis stressing "concern for production."

Using their grid, Blake and Mouton identify five major leader styles: a "country club" leader who concentrates only on people, a "production pusher" who pursues goals at all costs, a "do-nothing" leader who stresses neither people nor production, an "organization man" who settles for half a loaf and divides his energies between people and products, and the "team builder" who is committed to both people and production. Not surprisingly, Blake

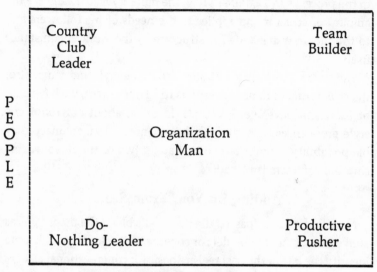

Country Club Leader	Team Builder
Organization Man	
Do- Nothing Leader	Productive Pusher

PEOPLE

PRODUCTION

and Mouton press leaders to adopt the team builder emphasis on both people and production as the single best leader style.

Most research agrees that both people and production are vital to healthy organizations. That same body of research shies away from trying to sell one style as consistently the best leader approach. Flexible use of several styles allows leaders to relate effectively and appropriately to different kinds of followers and to a range of work demands.

Where are your leader priorities? People? Production? Both? Neither?

How Does Your Leader Style Fit Congregational Needs?

Organizational leadership basically calls for meshing three factors: the leader's style, the follower's style, and the demands of the work situation itself. Daniel Tagliere has studied the leadership mesh process closely and spotlights structure as the key variable in the process.[6] In Tagliere's view, the ministry leader can vary the amount of structure he applies to the needs of his followers and to the inherent demands for structure in the work circumstance itself.

Since we leaders can select our own leader style and can control the structuring of ministry settings to a large extent, we have a lot of leadership leverage. We can't do much about our followers' style preferences without deliberate manipulation, an unacceptable possibility for minsters. But shaping two of the three leadership mesh factors isn't bad!

Adding Up Your Exam Score

Now that you've "passed the test," let's blend the theory pieces above into a coherent model for congregational leadership. Let me identify the bits of theory I feel are basic for congregational leadership. First, I agree with Burns that transforming leadership is preferred, especially at the top levels of organizational life. Second, it seems to me that most congregational leaders are emergent or servant in type.

Third, with Barber I suspect that effective leaders are active "people approachers" and are positively involved in discovering and implementing congregation-wide goals.

Fourth, I agree with Blake and Mouton that the people and production tensions are basic to organizational life. I further suggest that integrating, rather than simply balancing, a congregation's concerns for people and production makes for healthy congregations. Some leader-style flexibility, therefore, is necessary to integrate relationships and goals and to keep the leadership mix working well.

Finally, I feel strongly that effective congregational leaders treat their followers in ways that take the particular interests and needs of each follower seriously. Additionally, good leaders deal with varying ministry demands differently and wisely.

A Model of Congregational Leadership

Using these various pieces of information, four major leader-style options can be identified.[7] A model of congregational leadership emerges spotlighting the Catalyst, Commander, Encourager, and Hermit leaders. Here's a picture of a congregational leadership model holding in creative tension the congregation's mission, a basic institutional concern, and members' varied needs—a fundamental element in morale development. Notice that each of the leadership models in chapters 1 and 4 incorporates two dynamics: the congregation's health and the individual member's motives.

Describing Primary Leader Options

"If the only tool you have is a hammer, you tend to see every problem as a nail," according to Abraham Maslow. It's easy to fall into a leader-style rut. We tend to do the same things in the same ways with different people and in different circumstances. Even when our approach doesn't work well for us or others, we may press on anyway using a limited range of behaviors. Ruts become comfortable.

Here's a suggestion: look at leader styles as a smorgasbord—an almost infinite range of options. You'll feel more "elbow room" and freedom when you realize that you have many possibilities to choose from.

Here's another suggestion: consider each of the four primary styles I'll describe as a continuum. To illustrate, the Commander style, like the other options, exhibits a variety of temperaments. Commanders range from the warm, grandfatherly types (sometimes called the benevolent dictators) to absolute tyrants. In other words, there are several flavorings of leadership within each style.

I'll describe each leader style in stark terms. Sometimes I'll approach caricaturing the type in order to make a point. Remember that none of us represents a "pure" form of any of these styles. We're all probably a mixture of styles because of our varied experiences and backgrounds. In fact, at times I've personally used each of the styles I'll describe. You probably have too.

I have a personal preference based both on theology and experience. I feel the Catalyst style fits more kinds of followers and ministry situations comfortably than the other options. The Catalyst's balance and flexibility provides breadth. Therefore, I feel the Catalyst style is generally superior as an ongoing, day-in and day-out style option.

Each style, though, fits some situations particularly well and is especially usable in those situations. Later in the book I'll identify these special circumstances calling for a creative meshing of styles and other factors.

Catalyst: the Effective Style

In chemistry, a catalyst is an accelerant. Catalysts cause and/or speed up reactions but aren't consumed by the reactions themselves. Catalysts participate in the chemical process by providing a pathway for more rapid responses.

In leadership, the active-positive Catalyst style also creates pathways and processes which enhance the end result. Savor these synonyms for the Catalyst leader's style and behaviors: triggers action; a mover; participative; team captain; proactive; guides and trusts processes; balanced; developer; leads democratically; delegates comfortably; integrates members' needs and the mission of the congregation. Have you seen this style in yourself and others?

The Catalyst is a strong leader who gets results by involving people. To use Trueblood's phrase, he's a "playing coach."[8] He works with people and through people. At the same time, he keeps a vision of the congregation's mission cleanly defined and clearly communicated.

Theologically stated, the Catalyst believes grace has made a fundamental difference in his congregational members' lives. He sees potential in them and trusts them. The Catalyst is committed to helping his followers grow into leaders. Therefore, he equips them to grow and lead (see Eph. 4:11-13).

CONGREGATIONAL LEADERSHIP MODEL
Emphasizing CONGREGATIONAL MISSION

	Positive	Negative
Active	CATALYST Active/ Positive	COMMANDER Active/ Negative
Passive	Passive/ Positive ENCOURAGER	Passive/ Negative HERMIT

Emphasizing MEMBERS' NEEDS

Recently, a Tennessee church called a new staff member. In a letter to his congregation, the pastor affirmed,

> I've been pastor of this church for almost nine years, and I've never known this church to make a bad decision. . . . When you as a church are given all the information and an appropriate opportunity to discuss an issue, you always (in my judgment) make the right decision.

I see a Catalyst at work in this statement. This pastor trusts his people and the congregational processes.

I've closely observed the ministry of a Catalyst leader for two decades. An interesting pattern has developed. Each of his pastorates has experienced consistent numerical growth. That's impressive, since he's worked in a variety of favorable and unfavorable settings. What's more impressive to me is what's happened after he left each church. The growth remained stable. This Catalyst pastor builds up people, and they build up the congregation. He activates, teaches, strengthens, and helps his members gain maturity and confidence. Then, they become leaders in their own right.

Incidentally, this pastor gains influence by empowering others. His members appreciate being asked real questions, being listened to, hearing "thanks" said to them, and being included in the dreaming and planning processes. Therefore, they support what they've created. Their increased power doesn't diminish the Catalyst's self-image or power.

Why Is the Catalyst Style Effective?

• It's active. The Catalyst takes initiative. He's a people approacher.

• It's positive. The Catalyst keeps group energy focused on the basic mission of the congregation.

• It's balanced. The Catalyst integrates members' needs and the fundamental mission of his congregation.

• It's flexible. The Catalyst style meshes well with lots of follower personalities and many different circumstances.

• It's long-range. The Catalyst patiently builds for the long haul. Today is his work arena, but eternity's his time horizon.

The Catalyst must pay the demanding price of developing a full array of relational and organizational skills. This assortment of abilities creates high levels of effectiveness.

Commander: the Efficient Style

The Commander leaves no doubt about what he expects from his followers. Because of his interest in production, task, and structure, he gives them their orders of the day. They either comply or leave. That's efficiency by one definition.

I'm not suggesting that active-negative Commanders are always harsh. I know a Commander pastor who served the same congregation for thirty years. In actuality, he almost "became" the church. On one occasion, a member family complained about something the pastor had done. He invited them to his study, made them comfortable, and then said, "I hear that you're disappointed with my pastoral approach. It breaks my heart when members of my flock are unhappy. Tell me, where would you like for me to transfer your church membership?" This pastor was caring and courtly but a Commander all the way!

The Commander views people as lazy, uncreative, and only partially converted. Therefore, he must provide structure, ideas, and motivation for his followers. The Commander's use of high structure fits a few circumstances appropriately—but only a few.

Commanders may become "power wielders" who "rule by fear. These are the drivers who march *behind* their people."[9] Their confidence shades over into arrogance, in some cases. The Commander may even assume that God speaks more often and more directly to him than to other congregational members. Therefore, he may set the goals, call the shots, and bulldoze people as he feels the necessity. To use an extreme illustration, the apparently easygoing

Herbert Hoover once observed that a "President should have the right to shoot at least two people a year without explanation."[10]

Commanders emphasize goals more than relationships. They rigidly keep the pressure on, and sometimes they catch the backlash from their pressure. Let me illustrate that phenomenon with an incident out of my own ministry.

After a church business conference, a young married couple, new members of our congregation, approached me. "What happened in that meeting?" they demanded emotionally.

I reviewed the conference mentally and concluded it had been a fairly typical meeting for Baptists in the Midwest. "What seemed unusual?" I inquired.

"Several different people made motions. Folks debated viewpoints. When we voted, there were even a few negative votes. Then we sang and prayed together, and everyone left happy. We've never seen a church meeting like that before. What happened?"

I was still puzzled. "Can you tell me about the meetings you've seen?"

Their background was clarified by their answer: "Our pastor of eighteen years moderated the meetings and made all of the motions himself. Only deacons spoke up; they only seconded motions as previously arranged. There were no debates and no negative votes."

Now I realized this couple had grown up in an independent church with a Commander-styled leader. But "no negative votes?"

"No."

"Never?"

"Never." Then, after a long pause and a glance at each other, the young man admitted: "Well, there were negative votes once."

"When?" I asked them.

"The night the church split! The night the pastor had to resign!"

The price of efficiency is high when people feel used and abused. The active-negative leader approaches people easily. However, his negativity involves pressing his own goals on others rather than developing and guiding congregational goals. He imposes his personal mission on the group; in a congregational setting, that's generally negative.

Conflicts and ruffled feelings can be suppressed for only so long. Then, an explosion is likely, and someone—leader or follower—is apt to leave the congregation.

Why Is the Commander Style Efficient?

● It's clearly defined. Everyone knows what's expected. They either obey the Commander or exit.

● It has a narrow agenda. The Commander's goals are paramount.

● It's rigid. That is, followers always know what their task is and who's in charge.

● It's short-range. Quick results are possible and likely when the Commander style is used. However, people may not be trained for confident service later.

Encourager: the Empathetic Style

The Encourager stresses feelings and fellowship. He has honed his relational skills to the neglect of his organizational abilities. He may use his relational skills privately and counsel well. Or he may have mastered his public relations skills and preach well. In any event, people are his forte; goals are a necessary evil for him.

Several word snapshots describe the passive-positive Encourager: warm and trusting; helpful and conciliatory; approachable; works best one to one or one to a few; attentive; peacemaker; low production orientation; gives confidence to others. Is the Encourager style familiar to you?

A pastor friend describes his approach to ministry as a "high stroke" style. He's very charming. He nurtures, smiles, and greets people warmly. The truth is that he enjoys people (and dreads desk work and study disciplines). This Encourager spends a lot of time at pastoral tasks which pastors with different styles give a lower priority. He attends to people well and mediates differences comfortably. Metaphorically, the Encourager is a hand holder, a head patter, and a fence mender.

When the congregation needs an emotional change of pace, call in the Encourager. Tense conflicts or congregations grieving in the interim between pastors are natural settings for the Encourager to work his magic. He enriches fellowship, heals, smoothes troubled waters, binds people together, listens and undergirds, and provides a moratorium when the pressure of production is lessened. For the Encourager, people are the major agenda.

Why Is the Encourager Style Empathetic?

- It's person-centered.
- It low keys production. Therefore, it doesn't divide the leader's focus.
- It's valuable in congregations experiencing conflict and to persons feeling stressed.

Hermit: the Eroding Style

The Hermit withdraws from leader situations, closes his door, and asks to be left undisturbed. Even when he's in a staff or committee meeting, he secludes himself emotionally. A passive-negative Hermit rarely does today what he can put off until tomorrow. Ultimately, the Hermit's passivity creates a leadership vacuum. Unless lay leaders take initiative, the Hermit's church soon becomes inert.

A friend with Hermit tendencies described his concept of ministry to me: "Ideally, a pastor is the congregation's resident philosopher. He reads big books and preaches thoughtful sermons." Like the overstudious minister who was "invisible Monday through Saturday and incomprehensible on Sunday," the classic Hermit is seldom effective at the people-to-people and heart-to-heart work of ministry. A Hermit usually isn't comfortable enough with folks to enjoy the relational work of ministry.

Natural-born Hermits are shy and self-effacing around people. Timid Hermits are fairly common. After all, 40 percent of Americans consider themselves shy.[11] Timid people are easily spotted by others. Oddly, these shy types are rarely aware of how they come across to others.

Shyness primarily impacts first encounters. When strangers finally become known, the shy person relates well, listens patiently, and forms durable friendships. Time, maturity, and a sense of God's direction can help the shy Hermit cope with his style.

The Hermit style may also be the consequence of being crushed by a congregation. Consider this parallel. In the days of the sailing ships, some vessels seemed jinxed. These ships had rough voyages, accidents, and fatalities. When these so-called "widow makers" were paid for, they were deliberately scuttled. Some congregations may be widow makers too. When a pastor has been abused by such a group, he needs a caring and patient congregation where he can regain his confidence and rebuild his trust in God's people.

Why Does This Style Erode the Hermit and the Congregation?

- It's uncomfortable for the Hermit to approach people.
- It's unproductive when congregational goals aren't pursued.
- It undercuts confidence when neither relationships nor production are successfully met.

Exploring These Leader Styles

Let me sum up and compare these four congregational leader styles. The Catalyst is a fraternal leader who says, "We!" The Commander is a paternal leader who says, "Me!" The Encourager is a maternal leader who says, "Thee!" The Hermit is an external leader who says, "Why me?"

Other contrasts help identify our basic leader style options. The Catalyst both gives to and takes from others and the congregation. The Commander primarily takes. The Encourager mostly gives. The Hermit neither gives nor takes. Catalysts, Commanders, Encouragers, and Hermits—they're common to congregations.

CONGREGATIONAL LEADER-STYLE OVERVIEW

LEADER STYLE OPTIONS	Personality Mix	Basic Role	Primary Behaviors	Energy Focus	Major Outcome	Advantages & Disadvantages
CATALYST	Active-Positive	Participative	• Leads democratically. • Integrates persons and goals. • Activates, trains, organizes, & delegates.	Results	Long-term stability	+Long-range effectiveness. +Flexible relationally and situationally. •••••• −Demands a wide range of leader skills. −Requires time & member talent.
COMMANDER	Active-Negative	Directive	• Leads autocratically. • Puts goals before persons. • Directs, guides, demands, & presses.	Production	Quick response	+Efficient for short-term. +Gets things done fast. •••••••• −Creates pressure and conflict. −Becomes rigid.
ENCOURAGER	Passive-Positive	Nondirective	• Leads permissively. • Places persons before goals. • Nurtures, empathizes, mediates, and soothes.	Morale	Fellowship development	+Binds people together. +Creates relaxed atmosphere. •••••••• −Organization untended. −Tangible production wanes.
HERMIT	Passive-Negative	Submissive	• Leads passively. • Focuses on neither persons nor goals. • Withdraws, postpones, and retreats.	Safety	Inertia	+Buys time for organizational decision making. +Allows leader some time out of the fray. •••••• −Nothing happens. −Leaves leader vulnerable.

Notes

1 James MacGregor Burns, *Leadership* (New York: Harper and Row, 1978), p. 4.

2 *Ibid.*, p. 20.

3 Ralph M. Stogdill, *Handbook of Leadership: A Survey of Theory and Research* (New York: Free Press, 1974), pp. 121-146.

4 James David Barber, *The Presidential Character: Predicting Performance in the White House* (Englewood Cliffs, NJ: Prentice-Hall, 1977), James D. Barber, "Adult Identity and Presidential Style: The Rhetorical Emphasis," *Philosophers and Kings: Studies in Leadership*, ed. Dankwart A. Rustow (New York: George Braziller, 1970), pp. 367-397, and Angelia Herrin, "Probing the Presidency," *Raleigh (NC) News and Observer*, 2 November 1980, Sec. 4, pp. 1, 7.

5 Robert R. Blake and Jane S. Mouton, *The New Managerial Grid* (Houston: Gulf Publishing, 1978) and Robert Blake and Jane Srygley Mouton, "Should You Teach There's Only One Best Way to Manage," *Training/HRD*, April 1978, pp. 24-29.

6 Daniel A. Tagliere, *People, Power, and Organization* (New York: AMACOM, 1973).

7 I've attempted a similar description of leader styles in earlier writings. See Robert D. Dale, "Leader Style and Church Staff Mesh: Solving People Puzzles," *Review and Expositor* 78 (Winter 1981): 17-20.

8 Elton Trueblood, *The Incendiary Fellowship* (New York: Harper and Row, 1967), p. 43.

9 James MacGregor Burns, "True Leadership," *Psychology Today*, October 1978, p. 48 and James L. Hayes, *Memos for Management: Leadership* (New York: AMACOM, 1983), p. 12.

10 Hugh Sidey, "Taking Notes for History," *Time*, 28 Feb. 1983, p. 24.

11 "Timid Traits," *Raleigh (NC) Times*, 31 Aug. 1983, p. 4-B.

2
Roots: Where Does Your Style Come From?

In Middle Tennessee near the Kentucky border, the Cumberland and Obed Rivers flow together. One spring I saw an unusual sight from the bridge above the spot where these rivers join. The Cumberland was rolling south out of the Kentucky farmlands gorged with chocolate brown silt. The aqua green Obed was skipping down quickly from the mountains to the east. From atop the bridge I could see the two rivers squeezing into one river bed. The Cumberland side was muddy and brown while the Obed was green and almost clear. This striking pattern of two separate rivers crowding into one bed continued for several hundred yards. Then, the mixing process started, first with streaks of brown and green and finally with a complete blending of waters moving on toward Nashville.

Leader styles develop similarly. Diverse streams of life and experience flow together, intermingle naturally, and merge into a new whole. Home backgrounds, mentors and heroes, congregational climates, regional influences, and a variety of personal and psychological traditions all blend into our leader styles. Many of these factors converge so naturally and quietly we hardly notice the new rivers they create in our ministries.

Parents: Leader Makers

Home backgrounds are powerful shapers of leaders and their styles. Elton Trueblood claims religion is more caught than taught. The same may be true for leadership too. We learn how to take responsibility, deal with people, and exercise initiative by observing our parents and other authority figures. They become our models for living and leading.

T. B. Maston is probably Southern Baptists' best known ethicist. He taught eight to ten thousand students before he retired. He has written a score of books and numerous articles. In 1977 all three of the top elected officers of the Southern Baptist Convention were doctoral graduates with majors under Maston.

What are the roots of Maston's personal leadership influence? Teachers with whom he studied while earning two doctorates in religious studies? Outstanding faculty colleagues? No. In a letter to his father, Maston thanked God for the opportunity he had to work with his father on their East Tennessee family farm.

> I learned more Bible and doctrine from you during those years than from any teacher I have had since in college or seminary. And in what was more important I think I caught something of your spirit. I never can forget or get away from the influence of those chats we used to have at the end of the corn rows, when we talked about the most serious problems of the universe and the deepest possible religious problems.[1]

Like father, like son. Maston continued the "serious chat" approach in his teaching, writing, and relating.

Anna Wright, the mother of Frank Lloyd Wright, was so sure she was carrying a son before Frank's birth that she chose his profession in advance. Making up her mind that he would become an architect, she hung framed engravings of the world's greatest cathedrals in his nursery and supplied blocks and cardboard shapes for his first toys. Maybe she was following Freud's idea: "A man who has been the indisputable favorite of his mother keeps for life the feeling of a conqueror, that confidence of success that often induces real success."[2] From whatever combination of influences, Frank Lloyd Wright became an undisputed leader in the American architectural community during the middle years of this century.

Jimmy Carter was influenced by his father and still speaks of his father as if he's present although James Earl Carter, Sr., has been dead for thirty years. The elder Carter was a bespectacled, jowly man of average height with thinning hair. Yet when asked to describe his father, Jimmy Carter remembered him as big and powerful—rural royalty—larger than life. "Daddy's little man" grew up to be president with his father as a primary leader model.

Throughout our lives we draw on our parents' example of leadership. We may model after the persons we've loved and been shaped by so completely that choosing updated or fitting styles later becomes very difficult. In any event, their shaping influences include our leader styles too.

Mentors: Concrete Models of "How To"

Our mentors also provide concrete leadership models of how to do our work. Mentors sponsor us, guide us, teach us, adopt us; and they relate to us personally and professionally. Our mentors believe in us and help us believe in ourselves. They give us our professional birthright.

The Bible is full of mentoring relationships: Abraham for Lot; Jethro for Moses; Elijah for Elisha; Jesus for Peter, James, and John; Barnabas for Paul and John Mark; Paul for Silas and Timothy. Mentors provide opportunities and experiences for us. They demonstrate how to minister, and we mimic them.

The same mentoring process is true for other professions as well. Thomas Jefferson was mentored by George Wythe, a Williamsburg lawyer.[3] Jefferson understudied in Wythe's law office. This experience of being guided and nurtured by a prominent leader, a signer of the Declaration of Independence and a member of the Constitutional Convention, launched Jefferson into a place in history.

Following Wythe's advice, Thomas Jefferson stayed in Virginia during the Revolutionary War and served in the Virginia legislature. He would wrestle with the issues of public service at Williamsburg until exhausted, ride back to Monticello, rest and draft some more statutes, and then return to the legislative fray. During this period Jefferson proposed 150 statutes and successfully got fifty of them enacted, the most important one guaranteeing separation of church and state. George Wythe's stamp always remained on the life and work of Jefferson.

Mentors have already arrived professionally at where we want to go. We adopt their approach to leadership. Our mentors open doors for us, and we gladly and gratefully enter their world. Their leader style becomes one bedrock ingredient in the mix which produces our approach to ministry. Mentors allow us to watch them at work and, therefore, provide us with concrete models of leadership in congregational settings.

Congregational Climates and Leader Styles

Congregations develop their own "weather" or atmospheres. They are warm or cold, calm or stormy, quiet or thundery. In general, two major families of "ties that bind" are apparent in churches, according to a recent study of congregations.[4] Each climate implies a comfortable leader style.

"What you believe" church climates focus on ideology. These congregations stress doctrine, obligation, and indoctrination. Ministers seem to emphasize "what-you-believe" faith more than laypersons.

Members of ideological congregations tend to be articulate about their faith. They use "God talk" comfortably, especially slogans and religious jargon. Folks who are deeply ingrained in "what-you-believe" church climates tend to be less tolerant of others who don't share their viewpoints or who seem to deviate from ideological stances.

Ideological leaders tend to be more directive and stress doctrinal depth. Ideologues demand loyalty and keep their standards forcefully communicated. Old Testament prophets from the eighth century BC provide heroes for many ideologues.

"How you live" church climates focus on practical actions and attitudes. These congregations stress fellowship and supportive relation-

ships. Laypersons appear to fit the "how-you-live" mode better than ministers.

Members of behavioral congregations appreciate more diversity and religious pluralism. Their goal is to find and use sustaining relationships and resources for daily living.

Behavioral leaders tend to be more participative and emphasize community breadth. "How-you-live" leaders build an atmosphere of acceptance. The life and work of Christ commonly provides a model for behavioral faith.

Here's the crux of the matter. The type of church climate with which you're most familiar shapes your leader style. Ideological climates generally mesh well with directive leader styles and behavioral atmospheres with participative approaches.

Regionalism: Leaven for Leader Styles

"You are where you live," claims the demographer. Maybe so. It's true that leadership has a provincial flavor simply because it's always practiced in specific local settings. Different regions may call for different leader styles.

If you've lived or traveled in various parts of our nation, you know different regions have distinctive "feels" about them. Each area conveys attitudes and attributes of its people. Stereotypes also abound. For example: Vermonters are independent; Virginians are aristocratic; Missourians are stubborn; Texans are boastful; Californians are casual. Or so the popular wisdom claims.

Sociological studies have shown some personality differences across regions of the United States.[5] For example, Midwesterners have been found generally to fit their stereotypes: hardworking, conscientious, and stubbornly independent. No single personality trait, however, appears to be distinctive of our country at large. Several important lessons emerge here: (1) we're a diverse nation; (2) localities develop their own unique corporate personalities; (3) different leader styles may fit Oklahoma and Rhode Island or even East Tennessee and West Tennessee.

Regional Flavors and Style

Regions carry their own individual religious flavors too. For example, I grew up in a Protestant county in Missouri. We had one small, virtually invisible Catholic church in the county. Then the tables were turned on us completely. When I was twenty, my family moved to a predominantly Catholic New Mexico county with one Baptist church. My family immediately sensed a different religious atmosphere. My preteen brother met a cassocked priest on the street and rushed home to report, "Mom, I saw the Pope!" He didn't understand other religious groups because he didn't know them from firsthand experience.

A South Carolina Lutheran pastor found a gap in his seminary education. "Why didn't someone teach me how to survive in a Baptist county?" he complained. He had learned that some territories are so heavily populated by a single denomination that a virtual "state church" atmosphere prevails. Leader styles may respond, in part, to whether you're in the majority or minority.

Images of America and Style

Historically, three images have been used to characterize America: the Promised Land, the Frontier, and the Melting Pot.[6] Each image has created its unique institutions including churches. Each image also implies comfortable leadership styles.

Many settlers originally came to America in search of a new world, a promised land. Hope and the possibility of a fresh start characterize the promised land. The promised land is a blessed place, the dream of a better life. California is one example of the promised land for many, literally a Golden State. California was named by Spanish explorers in the sixteenth century after a treasure island in a then popular Spanish tale. Hollywood, America's dream merchant, holds out the possibility of stardom, a kind of permanent promise through the media.

Since paradise is heavenly, satisfaction is largely attained just by being in the promised land. Leader styles in the promised land tend to be relaxed and permissive. Institutional life is customarily optimistic and casual.

The frontier image of America overflows with the aura of youth and opportunity. For some, frontier means an escape from the constraints of tradition. For others, frontier smacks of the boldness required to conquer the unexplored. The frontier values independence, strength, confrontation, individualism, confidence, and competition.

Texas illustrates the frontier for many people. Likewise, the Texas Rangers symbolize one of the frontier spirit's most striking institutions. Famous for riding like Mexicans, trailing like Indians, shooting like Tennesseans, and fighting like the devil, the Rangers gained a rough-and-ready mystique. During a riot, an east Texas town called in the Rangers. When the train from Dallas arrived, only one Ranger got off. *Was a single peace officer enough?* the city fathers wondered. The Ranger calmly drawled, "Only one riot, ain't there?" That confidence and strength typifies frontier institutions.

Leaders influenced by the frontier image tend to become directive. They expect quick results and exhibit bravado, a militant individualism, and a near arrogance typical of the frontier and its institutions.

Diversity and pluralism are the hallmarks of the melting pot. In truth, virtually every American is either an immigrant or a descendant of an immigrant. The melting pot image recognizes that persons from diverse backgrounds have created a common culture with more similarities than differences. A key institution growing out of the melting pot is the public school where English language, history, and customs have been taught. Many persons who aren't comfortable with the melting pot aren't at ease with public schools either.

New York City offers one mirror of the melting pot. Consider the city's symbols: Statue of Liberty, United Nations headquarters, and Ellis Island. Listen to the ethnic flavor of New York's neighborhoods—Little Italy, Chinatown, Spanish Harlem, Bed-ford-Stuyvesant, Jamaica. Five ethnic groups—Irish, Italian, Jewish, Negro, and Puerto Rican—make up more than three fourths of the city's population. More recently, Los Angeles, and to a somewhat lesser extent Miami, have come to personify a new melting pot made up of Hispanics and Asiatics instead of Europeans.

Leaders in melting pot settings are usually participative in style. Melting pot institutions show that differences can be enriching. Diversity is encouraged and invited.

Merging Streams

How the diverse shapers of style come together in leaders has both unpredictable and predictable elements. The impact of parents and mentors is too varied to draw direct style implications. The congregational climates and images of America do suggest some predictable style implications for us, however.

The roots of our leadership styles converge from various sources. These streams of influence which merge in us and create our leader styles call for two personal reactions. First, we can identify and better understand the varied forces shaping us. Second, we can choose aspects of our roots to affirm. The merging process is lifelong because the streams continue to move within us.

Notes

1 Quoted in William M. Pinson's compilation, *An Approach to Christian Ethics: The Life, Contribution, and Thought of T. B. Maston* (Nashville: Broadman Press, 1979), p. 18.

2 David McCullogh, "Mama's Boys," *Psychology Today,* Mar. 1983, p. 38.

3 Robert K. Greenleaf, *Servant Leadership,* (New York: Paulist Press, 1977) pp. 30-32. See also Ross Arkell Weffer, "Managers & Heroes," *Management Review,* May 1980, pp. 43-45 and Daniel J. Levinson, et al, *The Seasons of a Man's Life* (New York: Alfred A. Knopf, 1978, pp. 218-222, 275. For an unpublished research project on role models in corporate life, investigate the Research Sponsors Program at the Center for Creative Leadership in Greensboro, NC.

4 Roger A. Johnson, *Congregations as Nurturing Communities* (Philadelphia: Division of Parish Services, Lutheran Church of America, 1979). Johnson's descriptions are reminiscent of Ernst Troeltsch's church and sect types of Christian organization

LEADER STYLE INFLUENCERS

	Directive Leaders	Participative Leaders	Permissive Leaders
Parents		Leader style varies with parental approach.	
Mentors		Leader style depends on mentor's modeling.	
Congregational Climates	Ideological Styles	Behavioral Styles	
Images of America	Frontier	Melting Pot	Promised Land

with structures based on their attitudes toward the cultural environment. For a secular treatment of organizational climate, see Terrence E. Deal and Allan A. Kennedy, *Corporate Cultures: the Rites and Rituals of Corporate Culture* (Reading, MA: Addison-Wesley, 1982).

5 Samuel E. Koug and Raymond W. Kulhavy, "Personality Differences across Regions of the United States," *Journal of Social Psychology,* 91 (1973), 73-79.

6 For a religious perspective on American character, see Sidney E. Ahlstrom's *A Religious History of the American People* (New Haven and London: Yale University Press, 1972). For a secular view on the subject, see Michael McGiffert, ed., *The Character of Americans* (Homewood: Dorsey Press, 1964). The importance of the image of the frontier in American development was stressed in Frederick Jackson Turner's 1893 paper on "The Significance of the Frontier in American History." Turner claimed the frontier had been the one great determinant of American culture, departing from earlier historians who had stressed the continuity of American institutions with Europe. The theme of America as blessed was expressed in the "manifest destiny" concept. Building on the Puritan sense of divine mission and the colonial charters which projected American territory from "sea to sea," the idea of the right of America to extend its boundaries became post-Civil War orthodoxy. Philosophies of imperialism, optimism, idealism, and perfectionism rode this crest. Will Herberg's *Protestant-Catholic-Jew,* new rev. ed. (Garden City, NY: Doubleday and Company, Inc., Anchor Books, 1960) provides a classic religious treatment of the melting pot metaphor.

3
Beliefs: Theology and Leader Style

Leader style grows out of our beliefs. Several seedbeds for the development of our styles are especially crucial for congregational leadership. Our views of human nature, biblical leaders' examples, and denominational traditions are basic shapers of leader style.

Spelling M-A-N

In Eugene O'Neill's play *The Great God Brown,* the main character, Brown, lies dead on the street. A policeman bends over Brown's body and asks, "What's his name?" A bystander responds, "Man." The policeman concentrates on his notebook and with pencil poised asks, "How do you spell it?"

M-A-N. How I "spell" man is a key issue for me as a leader. If I have a low estimate of humanity, I'll tend to rule with an iron hand. Why not? These dolts need all the help they can get! If, on the other hand, I see people as basically gifted and willing to exercise their ministries through the church, I'll tend to give them support and latitude. My leader style grows out of my estimate of human nature.[1] In fact, my leader style is the most direct ministry application of my doctrine of humanity.

How the Bible, theology, and church history have spelled man provides a basic beginning point for leaders. Personally, I see the Bible making at least four major affirmations about human nature. Each "spelling" has implications for leader styles.

Mankind is spelled C-R-E-A-T-U-R-E. The creation story describes man as made of common stuff like the rest of the universe.

But there's one gigantic difference. We're created by God in his image—*image Dei,* as theologians describe it. We're special.

The image of God in us is a rich, multidimensional idea. Human beings are stewards of creation (Gen. 1:26-27; Ps. 8:3-6). We're also relational. We need others (Gen. 2:18-25) and long for fellowship with God. Finally, man can respond to God and others. This dynamic concept sees God as addressable and man as answerable.

Human beings are both finite and free. Leaders see the potential in people and work to call out their special gifts for service. The image of God in persons suggests we can approach followers with confidence.

Additionally, mankind is spelled S-I-N-N-E-R. The Bible states the fact starkly, "All have sinned" (Rom. 3:23). Human sinfulness is a universal reality resulting from man's misdirected free choice (Gen. 3:1-6). God didn't (and doesn't) force man to sin; man's options remain open. The old Flip Wilson line "The Devil made me do it!" won't change the truth: man chose (and chooses) to sin.

Traditionally, theologians have pinpointed the root sins as pride —overstepping our limits—and apathy, underestimating our potential. Whether launched from pride or apathy, all sin is bad. Interpersonal sins, however, are especially reprehensible. Others become enmeshed in the rippling impacts of social sin (1 Cor. 6:18).

Leaders must be alert to the impacts of sin on ourselves and those whom we try to lead. We, leaders and followers, are always contaminated choicemakers. We need self-discipline as well as others' support and confrontation.

Humankind is also spelled N-E-W C-R-E-A-T-I-O-N. The New Testament uses a number of different images to describe the new life of the Christian person.

Jesus in the Synoptic Gospels refers to believers as disciples or learners. To be re-created by Christ calls us to abandon sin, shoulder crosses, slash home ties, face the glares and stones of tradition's bigots, buddy with outcasts and cheats and corpses, and die in disgrace—a total bust when measured on the "organization man's" success scale. It is the most radical life possible.

John claims that because of the new birth (John 3) Christians have eternal life. It means believing with your head, heart, and hands. It calls us to set self aside and stick to a God kind of life. It is the best life possible.

Paul's favorite phrase for the new creation (2 Cor. 5:17) is "in Christ." It means a union of the penitent's life with Christ's, growth from babyness to adulthood, and pursuing the goal of godliness. It is the most challenging life possible.

The Book of Acts emphasizes the community of the Holy Spirit the Christian belongs to. The General Epistle to the Hebrews uses the pilgrim image to convey the growth process ingrained in the Christian's life. It is the most difficult life possible.

Leaders stay aware of the purpose and power we experience as Christ's new creations. We help followers channel their motivation constructively. The possibilities for exciting service are endless.

Finally, theology spells man P-I-L-G-R-I-M. The Christian is on the move because he follows a trailblazing, pacesetting God. The Christian faith pursues a distinctive pathway. The ancient Greeks claimed man is what he thinks. Karl Marx said man is what he consumes. But Christ changed the focus of living. Jesus taught that people are what they love. The goal of Christian love draws us forward toward Christ and others.

Leaders help followers sense their stewardship and opportunities. Christians are growers, living in response to God's love and living in responsible love with others. We thrive on challenge.

Types of Old Testament Leaders

A brief survey of biblical-leader types pinpoints a variety of leadership approaches. Each leader category models style possibilities. Throughout the biblical record, God consistently searched for a variety of quality leaders. First Samuel 13:14 makes the point: "The Lord has sought out a man after his own heart; and the Lord has appointed him to be prince over his people."

In the Old Testament, a rich range of leaders emerges. Some of these types are, in an organizational sense, minor and others major. *Prophets and prophetesses* are highly visible biblical leaders. These reformers overlapped into both religious and political issues. Their leader styles weren't developed in organizational settings and, therefore, are difficult to translate without major modification into today's local church settings.

Another Old Testament leader type was the *priest*. These worship leaders specialized primarily in religious ceremonies. And, for the most part, they led in a quiet manner.

The *kings* were leaders on a national scale. They were seen as God's representatives, an important distinction. Unlike other Oriental monarchs, the kings of Israel weren't dictators who exercised unchecked control over their subjects. From its beginning the nation Israel was a theocratic confederation, a religious and moral community with God as their actual king. Religion, then, was the basic authority rather than a king, a political organization, or a national governmental structure.

The kingly role itself was likely an extension of the head of the tribe or of the seventy elders chosen by Moses to assist in national leadership. Saul was chosen by God to be his first kingly representative. But Saul's power wasn't absolute. Israel's tradition provided a primitive system of checks and balances. The king's authority was somewhat limited on the religious side by the prophets and priests and on the political side by the tribal chiefs.

But Israel's future as a nation didn't depend on political prominence. Faithful fulfillment of God's missionary purpose for them defined their opportunity for greatness. Israel was created to become a servant nation. Within this mission, the king was to guide the nation toward its covenant destiny under God.

The *judges* were temporary leaders who helped deliver the local clans from destructive cycles of sin and idolatrous behavior. The period of the judges was a continuing struggle between Israel's desert religion and Canaan's native religion. During this early period of Hebrew history, some of the Israelites were enticed by the novelty, "sophistication," and gaudy festivals of Baal worship (Judg. 6:25-36).

Several features of the judges' leadership situation were unique to them. For instance, these men and women were military heroes and heroines, not officers of law. Additionally, they were local and tribal rather than national, temporary rather than permanent or hereditary, inspirational personalities rather than royal figures, and concurrent, not consecutive, leaders.

A cycle of sin, oppression, deliverance, and faithfulness repeats itself throughout the history of the judges. Note the four-step process. Without a judge, Israel fell into Baal worship (Judg. 2:11-13,19). Idolatry brought oppression on the unfaithful (Judg. 2:14-15). Then, God would call a judge who would deliver Israel (Judg. 2:16-18a). Finally, the cycle would run its course with Israel remaining faithful to God while they were led by a judge (Judg. 2:18b).

The *sages* of the Old Testament were another group of important, although virtually invisible, leaders. They were the king's teachers. Using this crucial behind-the-scenes position, they molded the minds of the kings and other national leaders. The sage's power accumulated because he was near the center of government. As a group, the sages rose to prominence after the Exile and became equal in influence with the prophets and priests, who were fewer in number then. The sages also produced a body of biblical literature including the Proverbs, Job, Ecclesiastes, and selected Psalms (15, 111, and 112). Solomon, whose peaceful reign allowed time for thought, became the patron of sages.

Sages tended to be conservative, low-risk influencers. They did things the tried, tested, prudential way. For good or ill, for the first time Judaism under the sages moved toward becoming a world religion. The sages filled three basic functions: advising kings, teaching, and writing. Their philosophical literature emphasized two themes: the fear of God coupled with reflection on human experience. I once preached a sermon series from the Proverbs and called it "Heavenly Horse Sense" to capture these dual threads.

Several lessons about leadership can be gleaned from these Old Testament models. It's pivotal that religious leaders remember that we represent God; we serve God's redemptive mission in the world. Further, even leaders who are not "fulltime," like interim pastors and bivocational ministers, can exercise strong leadership. Finally, the sages remind us that behind-the-scenes advisors exert great influence in communities.

Models of Leadership in the New Testament

The New Testament provides additional interactive leadership models. Obviously, Jesus is the premier leader in the Bible. Although we are privileged to observe only a few over thirty days of his actual ministry in the pages of the New Testament, we see him leading through example and molding leaders by teaching them. Several themes emerge from studying Jesus' leader style.

Servant leadership was Jesus' basic approach. His commitment to service is plainly described in a classic passage on leader style: "For the Son of Man also came not to be served but to serve" (Mark 10:45). The British commander Lord Montgomery said his war experience had taught him that the military staff's role was to be the servant of troops in the field.

Jesus modeled *unambitious leadership.* The incarnation of Jesus— God becoming man in Jesus Christ—demonstrates a downward mobility. He emptied himself of divine rights and came to earth to redeem us. This approach stands in contrast to the American success formula of upward mobility. Ambition has always been a threat to religious leaders. For instance, Diotrephes, a visible member of the early church, is described as one "who likes to put himself first" (3 John 9).

Jesus also demonstrated *unauthoritarian leadership.* Jesus had authority but used it sparingly. His style was to love, not dominate. This spirit is seen elsewhere in the New Testament: pastors are warned not to lord it over or become domineering with their congregations (1 Pet. 5:3).

Other than Jesus, the New Testament speaks of several other groups of leaders. *Apostles,* for example, were mainly missionaries. These leaders had a special sense of "sentness." Not an office and not strictly limited to the twelve, these folks had seen Jesus and bore witness to his resurrection around the world (Matt. 28:19-20; Mark 16:15; Acts 1:8).

Pastors and deacons were local church leaders. Whatever role differences, if any, the early church intended, pastors and deacons had the same ministry functions. They were all called to proclaim the gospel, care for church and community members, and guide the congregation in fulfilling its purpose.

A well-known New Testament passage on leadership is Paul's list of qualifications for pastors and deacons (1 Tim. 3:1-13). Church leaders face heavy demands in both preparation and performance.

- They must have unimpeachable character.
- They must have unchallenged morals.
- They must be intellectually disciplined and able to teach others.
- They must maintain an open heart and an open house.
- They must be seasoned and proven church workers.
- They must be family leaders.
- They must relate to others well.
- They must have mastered their drives for money and position.

These brief suggestions about leadership in the New Testament remind us of several implications. Leaders in ministry have a missionary responsibility. To paraphrase John Wesley, the world is our parish. Further, a personal sense of calling is basic to religious leadership. Our primary role is to serve God and others. Finally, leaders in local congregations are expected to set the pace in a variety of ministry situations.

Tradition and Style: a Denominational Case Study

"History tells us how we got this way," asserted my history professor, the late E. W. Thornton. Each denomination has its distinctive history. How we got this way is especially important for large, scattered denominations like Southern Baptists.

Southern Baptists have a fascinating family tree. In some ways, the Southern Baptist Convention's nearly forty thousand churches and roughly 14 million members are like a huge elm with four taproots. In America we spring from at least a minimum of four root systems.[2] Our multiple taproots make for strength and durability; they also create variety and confusion. Moreover, each major Baptist tradition has yielded its own heroes and, consequently, its own variety of leader models.[3]

The Statesman Model:
Richard Furman (1755-1825) and the Charleston Tradition

Richard Furman's ministry grew out of Baptists' early roots in Charleston, South Carolina, and created the foundations for several bedrock Baptist organizations. Furman was born in New York state and grew up near Charleston and Columbia, South Carolina. His father was a pioneer teacher who tutored Richard in the classical disciplines.

Richard was converted under the preaching of a Separate Baptist minister and mentored by Oliver Hart, a Regular Baptist pastor in Charleston, merging both traditions in himself. Furman became a boy evangelist. At age thirty-two he assumed the pastorate of First Baptist Church in Charleston, the oldest Baptist congregation in the South since its founding around 1700.

Furman was an ardent patriot. He supported the American Revolution and joined other religious libertarians in disestablishing the Anglican Church in South Carolina. When Charleston fell to the British, Cornwallis placed a reward of 1,000 pounds sterling on Furman's head. He was forced to flee for two and a half years to North Carolina and Virginia where Patrick Henry attended Furman's congregation.

Richard Furman strongly advocated education. His thirteen surviving children including his daughters were given educations. Furman also pressed for the education of ministers. Furman University, the first Baptist college in the South, became one of his educational legacies.

Furman's greatest contribution to Baptist work was as an organizational statesman. He served as moderator of the Charleston Baptist Association, the oldest in the South, for twenty-five years and was president of the association's executive committee for thirty-four consecutive years. Furman helped organize the South's first Baptist state convention structure in South Carolina as well as the Triennial Convention in 1814. The Triennial Convention was the first organized effort by Baptists to support foreign missions; he served as the first president of this national Baptist body. Most important, Richard Furman proposed the "Convention Plan," a centralized polity guided by an executive committee and based on voluntary cooperation of member churches. Now the accepted practice of Southern Baptists, this arrangement was a tighter structure than the society model characteristic of Baptists in the North.

Richard Furman's leader style fit the Charleston tradition well. He was a courtly and dignified worship leader, predictable, an evangelistic Calvinist, a practical planner, and intellectually cultivated. Furman saw missions and education as primary tasks for every congregation and interdependence in ministry as the opportunity of all Baptist churches. Furman modeled denominational statesmanship for Baptists.

The Revivalist Model:
Shubal Stearns (1706-1771) and the Sandy Creek Tradition

Shubal Stearns, a native of Boston, was converted under the influence of George Whitefield's revivals and became a New Light preacher. Stearns then joined Baptists around mid-century.

He moved to Virginia, associated himself with the ministry of his brother-in-law, Daniel Marshall, but soon left Virginia in search of a freer religious atmosphere. Stearns settled in North Carolina southeast of the present Greensboro and in 1755 founded the Sandy Creek Baptist Church. This Separate Baptist group started with 16 members. Stearns was the pastor; Daniel Marshall served as one of two assistants. The result of this little band's evangelistic efforts was phenomenal. In 17 years, 42 churches and 125 ministers were launched into service by the Sandy Creek Church. The bivocational preachers of the Sandy Creek tradition made no advance sermon preparation, believing instead that God would supply them with a message.

Shubal Stearns was a leader who could inspire great loyalty. He was a powerful preacher, a committed Calvinist, a forceful personality, and a zealous evangelist. Stearns's tradition has yielded revivalistic preaching, informality in worship, fierce local church autonomy, and an antieducation stance. Stearns gave Baptists a revivalistic leader image.

The Crusader Model:
J. R. Graves (1820-1893) and the Landmark Tradition

The Tennessee tradition in Baptist backgrounds was the product of J. R. Graves. Born in Vermont and the youngest of three children, Graves's father died when J. R. was only two weeks old. Hard work left no time for formal schooling. When hired as a school teacher in his late teens, Graves had to study every night in order to stay ahead of his students' lessons for the next day.

Although his family's religious roots were in the Huguenot and Congregational traditions, Graves was converted to Baptist views at age fifteen. While teaching school in Kentucky later, the church where Graves was a member took steps to ordain him—without his consent. Eventually, Graves claimed a double calling—to ministry and to make war on doctrinal errors.

Graves moved to Nashville and began his career in religious journalism, cementing his image as a crusader and a controversialist. As an editor, he confronted Methodists, Campbellites, Catholics, and others who didn't conform to his beliefs.

In 1851 Graves began the Landmark Movement, an attempt to show an unbroken succession of Baptist churches extending back to New Testament times. Through his religious paper and his spellbinding preaching, he was able to make his doctrinal perspective dominant in the frontier southwest, mainly Tennessee, Mississippi, Louisana, Texas, and parts of several surrounding states.

A series of controversies—a libel conviction and fine, dismissal from the membership of Nashville's First Baptist Church, several abortive attempts to develop a Sunday School union and publish its literature, and disagreements with the Foreign Mission Board's missionary appointment process—drew both loyal supporters and bitter enemies around Graves. Finally, the Civil War, deaths of his mother and wife in a typhoid epidemic, bankruptcy of his publishing endeavors, and a stroke mellowed Graves considerably toward the end of his life and slowed Landmarkism's momentum. Landmarkism's divisive impact on Southern Baptist life lessened somewhat after 1905 when the Landmarks started their own denominational group.

Graves established a new leader image. He was a dominating speaker who could hold his listeners' rapt attention for two or three hours at a time. He preached with calm intensity but wrote in a more abrasive manner. Graves's temperament was energetic, magnetic, and rough-and-tumble. His Landmark ideas based on shaky historical grounds have left some suspicions about denominational institutions, kept Baptists from interdenominational cooperation, and undergirded the primacy of the local congregation. Graves demonstrated the crusader approach for Baptists.

The Loyalist Model:
I. T. Tichenor (1825-1902) and the Georgia Tradition

i. T. Tichenor, the son of a planter, began his ministry as the "Boy Orator of Kentucky" and later became a missionary to the Indians. He held pastorates in Mississippi and Tennessee as well as a fifteen-year stint at First Baptist Church in Montgomery, Alabama. Additionally, Tichenor served as president of a coal-mining company in Alabama and was nominated by Democrats to run for governor of Alabama, an opportunity he declined. When Alabama started an agricultural college at Auburn in 1872, Tichenor became president and professor of moral philosophy and served there for ten years.

Following the Civil War, Southern Baptists were so financially destitute that many Convention ministries faced extinction. For several years Baptists considered either closing their Home Mission Board or combining efforts with Northern Baptist's Home Mission Society. In 1879 the Convention strongly affirmed the need for the mission board. In 1882 Home Mission Board operations were moved from Marion, Alabama, to Atlanta; Tichenor was named to the top executive post. The challenge was literally to save Southern Baptist's home mission enterprise.

Tichenor was, however, a natural choice for the job—a missionary, a Southern patriot and a combatant at Shiloh, a denominationally active Baptist pastor, and an experienced business leader. He also proved to be a master persuader. Tichenor understood Baptists as well as the South's plight. He appealed to Southern Baptist's sense of loyalty, raised money ably, and showed himself a strong administrator. Tichenor was successful in establishing the Home Mission Board as an effective ministry agency.

Tichenor modeled leadership that was loyal to Baptists and the South. He stayed on fire for home missions. He related to all kinds of people easily, preached powerfully, remained optimistic, and knew when to push and when to let time become his ally. Under his leadership, the effort to evangelize America was vastly advanced, denominational loyalty increased, and southern sectionalism expanded. Tichenor modeled institutional loyalty for Baptists.

These four traditions, their heroes, and the models of leadership they represented still impact us. Much of the effect of these varied heroes is experienced unconsciously by current leaders as "the way Baptists have always operated." But Baptists who have

THEOLOGICAL PERSPECTIVES ON LEADER STYLES

	Directive Leaders	Participative Leaders	Permissive Leaders
Estimates of Human Nature	Pessimistic, emphasizes sin.		Optimistic, emphasizes salvation.
Biblical Leaders	Prophets	Kings Apostles, Pastors and Deacons	Sages	Priests
Denominational Models and Traditions	Crusaders	Revivalists	Statesmen	Loyalists

grown up predominately under the influence of one tradition may feel other leaders out of different Baptist traditions aren't legitimate members of the denomination.

Leadership Shaped by Belief

What we believe about human nature, biblical descriptions of leadership, and our denominational models provide some theological foundations for our practice of leadership. Theology is lived ultimately in ministry. Much of our theology is practiced in leadership.

Notes

1 Emil Brunner, *Man in Revolt* (Philadelphia: Westminster Press, 1947), p. 34

2 The four-tradition explanation of Baptist heritage is drawn from Walter B. Shurden's Carver-Barnes lecture, "The Southern Baptist Synthesis: Is It Cracking?," *Outlook* insert, Mar.-Apr. 1981, pp. 5-10 along with supplemental material from William L. Lumpkin, *Baptist Foundations in the South* (Nashville: Broadman Press, 1961). For additional information on Richard Furman, see Robert A. Baker, *The First Southern Baptists* (Nashville: Broadman Press, 1966); Robert A. Baker and Paul J. Craven, Jr., *Adventure in Faith: the First 300 Years of First Baptist Church, Charleston, South Carolina* (Nashville: Broadman Press, 1982); Loulie Latimer Owens, *Saints of Clay: the Shaping of South Carolina Baptists* (Columbia, SC: R. L. Bryan Company, 1971); and *Encyclopedia of Southern Baptists* 1958 ed., s.v. "Furman, Richard," by Winston C. Baff and Lynn E. May, Jr.

For additional information on Shubal Stearns, see *Encyclopedia of Southern Baptists*, 1958 ed., s.v. "Stearns, Shubal" by J. Allen Easley; Eugene Skelton, *A Walk in the Light* (Richmond: Skipworth Press, 1980).

For additional information on J. R. Graves, see O. L. Hailey, *J. R. Graves: Life, Times and Teaching* (Nashville: n. p., n.d.), James E. Tull, *Shapers of Baptist Thought* (Valley Forge: Judson Press, 1972), and *Encyclopedia of Southern Baptists*, 1958 ed., s.v. "Graves, James Robinson," by Homer L. Grice.

For additional information on I. T. Tichenor, see Joe W. Burton, *Road to Recovery* (Nashville: Broadman Press, 1977) and *Encyclopedia of Southern Baptists*, 1958 ed., s.v. "Tichenor, Isaac Taylor," by Kimball Johnson.

3 One characteristic of Southern Baptists is the tendency to personalize movements, issues, and controversies. I've chosen to build on that pattern by selecting a representative leader from each of four traditions. For additional information on the personalization of conflicts in Baptist history, see Walter Shurden, *Not a Silent People* (Nashville: Broadman Press, 1972).

II
Leaders, Followers, and Consequences

4
Matching Leader and Follower Styles

Congregations are naturally interactive communities of leaders and followers. A church, therefore, needs interactive leadership. "Inter"—with, mutual, between, among. "Active"—initiating, causing change, working. Interactive—working together, cooperating, acting on each other. An interactive atmosphere is basic to healthy congregational functioning.

Savor the "taste" of phrases and terms about interactive leadership: teamwork; mutual goals; social contract; shared values; a process of influence and counterinfluence; a dynamic relationship; mutual dependence and interdependence; a democratic community; group unity; the "consent of the governed"; a covenant relationship; a cohesive structure; the golden rule of reciprocity.

In an interactive setting, matching leader and follower styles is a major challenge. In churches, this match may be the key to effective and harmonious ministry efforts.

Follower Styles and Leadership

Followers also develop comfortable patterns of relating to congregations and leaders.[1] Follower styles, like leader styles, run the full gamut of emotional needs.

Remember the twin dynamics of institutional and individual concerns? For followers, congregations provide a community of meaning. That's the institutional dimension of followership. Either followers affiliate with the community for fellowship, or they draw meaning from the beliefs or mission of the congregation, or both. On the relational side of volunteer organizations, followers expect leaders to enrich their lives in some significant way.[2]

Leaders need followers. Like water seeking its own level, each leader style implies a reciprocal and complementary follower style. For instance, when the same four-style model of congregational leadership (see chapter 1) is applied to follower approaches, four follower styles emerge which mesh naturally with the basic leader types. Participants, Dependents, Receivers, and Self-Starters are typical responses of church members to the congregation as a community of meaning and to the leader as one who offers a life-enriching relationship.

Participants: the Catalyst's Preferred Followers

The Participant views the community of faith positively and purposefully. The congregation's clear sense of corporate vision is valued, supported, and shared by the Participant. On the relational side of the ledger, the Participant is enriched by active involve-

CONGREGATIONAL
FOLLOWER STYLE MODEL

Community of Meaning

E n r i c h i n g L i f e	PARTICIPANT (gains both meaning and enrichment from leader)	DEPENDENT (counts on leader for meaning primarily)
	RECEIVER (counts on leader for enrichment primarily)	SELF-STARTER (gains little meaning or enrichment from leader)

ment in the processes, programs, and relationships of the congregation. In fact, his involvement may be developing him into a leader within the congregation.

Participants are cooperative team players. They stay actively involved in congregational enterprises. Participants take responsibility. With the Catalyst, Participants join in the dreaming, making ministry decisions, setting goals, building the fellowship of the group, and implementing the congregation's mutual vision.

Dependents: the Commander's Preferred Followers

The Dependent is also clear about the vision of the church. However, because much of the mission of the congregation is the leader's own idea, a narrower perspective prevails than in a participative environment. In some cases, the congregation becomes so much clearer about what it's against than what it's for that an "anti" atmosphere develops, and straw men enemies are constructed and knocked down as an ongoing practice.

For the true Dependent, "follow the leader" is a way of life, not a game. Relationally, the Dependent leans heavily on the leader for definition. Relating to a particular leader or belonging to one specific congregation may provide some followers with their identity. Leaders may appeal to the Dependent based on the Commander's magnetic personality and charisma resulting in a "modern tribalism."[3]

On the more negative side, an "authoritarian dyad"[4] may develop. In this case, an unhealthy relationship emerges between a domineering leader and a helpless follower. The trade-off here is control and domination of the follower in return for the leader's protection from risk and responsibility. The long-term flaw in this style of relating is that the Dependent is never prepared to assume leadership roles.

Abdicrats invite autocrats to take the risks out of their lives. Dependents are uncomfortable with participative decision making and direct responsibility. They prefer to remain in the background of leadership settings. Dependents may be loyal lieutenants, but they prefer to derive their influence secondhand. They stay in less visible postures and act unassertively. In their most extreme forms, they invite domination and become puppetlike.

Unfortunately, neither the full-scale Commander nor the complete Dependent get what they want—an authentic relationship. Consider a historical illustration. Frederick the Great, the militaristic king of eighteenth-century Prussia, had one order for his subjects: "Obey!" Ironically, just before he died, he admitted, "I am tired of ruling slaves."[5] Commanders and Dependents mesh with each others' emotional needs, but neither of these types can establish or sustain equal relationships.

Receivers: the Encourager's Preferred Followers

Receivers depend on the congregation for the fellowship of a group they consider meaningful. Their loyalty to the congregation's broader purposes may be marginal, however. They count on the leader for an important relationship for enriching their lives. Receivers reach out to Encouragers for caretaking.[6] They are often needy and obedient, sometimes unrealistic, occasionally demanding, or even parasitic. "Take care of me," they ask leaders. Encouragers are seen by Receivers as successful belongers. The Encourager responds with charm, warmth, tact, concern, and sensitivity. Encouragers may succumb to Receiver's needs and become overprotective of them and spoil the Receivers. Like Dependents, Receivers don't grow into leaders either.

Self-Starters: the Hermit's Preferred Followers

The congregation offers Self-Starters sufficient meaning to remain linked to the tasks or fellowship of the congregation. The leader, however, offers little or nothing to his followers except a symbolic presence. He's like the pastor who introduced himself to me and, with a laugh, said, "I'm the guy who keeps Second Church from having a pastor." His put-down of himself may have indicated his Hermit-styled view of his leadership.

Self-Starters fill the leadership vacuum created by Hermits.

While the Hermit is officially designated the leader, in reality he often follows his followers. Hermits retreat, and the most assertive Self-Starters take action. Although the Hermit finds himself uncomfortable with the assurance and autonomy of the Self-Starter, he relies on the Self-Starter's ability to motivate himself and to exercise independent initiative.

The Growth of Followers

To sum up, followers can and do grow into leaders when they're given a developmental environment. Leaders can establish a climate in which followers over time can move into stronger, more balanced follower styles.

Another factor leaders must consider as a style issue is what the ministry situation itself demands. Each leader style suggests a preferred ministry situation.[7] These situations are also shaped by two dynamics: the congregation's institutional resources for ministry and the structure leaders add to ministry settings.

CONGREGATIONAL
MINISTRY
SITUATIONS MODEL

Organizational Resources

COOPERATIVE SITUATIONS (draws on both congregational resources and leader's structure)	UNSTABLE and OVERSTABLE SITUATIONS (relies on leader for organizational resources primarily)
ORDERLY SITUATIONS (relies on leader for helpful structure primarily)	SELF-SUSTAINING SITUATIONS (draws only marginally on congregational resources and leader's structure)

(left margin, vertical) S t r u c t u r i n g   H e l p

Cooperative Situations:
the Catalyst's Favored Settings

In Cooperative Situations the congregation carries its side of the bargain and offers plentiful resources for needed ministries. Relationally, the leader provides structure both for meeting member needs himself and for mobilizing other congregational members into mutual ministry networks. The Catalyst functions best in these settings.

Several congregational and member ingredients are necessary for the Catalyst and Cooperative Situations to merge creatively. A cadre of trained workers, enough time to let processes develop and people grow, and events calling for broad-based involvement provide a platform for the Catalyst's work to be most effective.

Unstable and Overstable Situations:
the Commander's Favored Settings

Commanders thrive on two vastly different settings: Unstable and Overstable Situations.[8] First, he works well in shaky situations demanding control. For example, when the ministry situation is confused and chaotic, the Commander style is effective. Remember how Jesus took direct control of a panicky situation and quieted the winds after the disciples had lost their composure (Mark 4:39)? When disorder and fear reign, the Commander style provides needed structure and stability.

Another situation fitting the Commander occurs when the congregation is stagnant, apathetic, stuck, or inert. Inertia, or overstability, is an organizational state as well as a physical one. Physicists, following Isaac Newton's lead, describe inertia as the property which makes motionless objects remain stationary until some force puts them into motion. The greater the mass of objects, the harder it is to put those objects into motion or to change their direction. Cases involving large or completely inert objects require additional time and effort to get them moving.

Ministry leaders encountering stuck congregations may need to adopt a directive style at least temporarily and give the motionless group a shove in a redemptive direction. Sometimes a nudge is necessary to confront apathy.

Other situational factors seem to suit the Commander style well. For instance, some denominations, ethnic groups, and geographic regions appear to favor the Commander leader style. These settings tilt toward directive leaders and dependent followers.

Orderly Situations:
the Encourager's Favored Settings

The Encourager, in order to excel in relational ministries, needs a congregation with stable, familiar organizational structures. With this organizational "track to run on," he can concentrate on creating a friendly, relaxed atmosphere. Where tradition directs programs almost automatically, there's room for comfortable members, depending on their needs and motives, either to pursue goals or to do nothing.

Because the Encourager prefers people concerns over production issues, he usually needs a talented cast of other leaders around him to be effective. Many Encouragers enjoy counseling and preaching and give low priority to administration and programming. However, a balanced staff of professional or lay ministers can help the congregation select and implement its ministry goals.

Self-Sustaining Situations:
the Hermit's Favored Settings

Self-Sustaining ministries and programs suit the Hermit's mindset. He likes to do a bare minimum of relational and institutional maintenance. If the congregation is in a self-perpetuating rut, the Hermit is more comfortable because institutional demands are lessened.

The Hermit style fits two leadership situations especially well. First, when a personal or congregational break is needed, a Hermit's retreating pattern permits batteries to be recharged. To illustrate, a devotional exercise I occasionally practice is to read the Gospel of Mark through at one sitting. It helps me examine Jesus' life and ministry systemically. I've noted how Mark shows graphically the temporary retreats of Jesus for rest and renewal. Jesus' ministry reveals a natural rhythm between intense activity and contemplation. An effective leader needs both a clear sense of purpose and the energy to pursue his goals.

Second, when the congregation is polarizing itself into a no-win stalemate, a short-term Hermit stance may be called for. If the group can agree to postpone an action in order to explore other alternatives actively, better solutions may be found. Time to think, pray, and explore options in a less emotionally charged setting can unfreeze dangerous situations. Pulling back doesn't solve the problem finally; it only buys time to search for other creative options.

Style Flex for Improved Effectiveness

Let's return to an inevitable question: What's the most effective leader style for ministers? In actual practice, it depends—on the congregational leader's style, the followers' style, and the demands of the ministry situation.

In some cases, the most comfortable mix of those three factors happens naturally.

In other cases, however, the meshing of factors must be adjusted deliberately, and perhaps temporarily, to accommodate special circumstances. This process of consciously matching personal

COMFORTABLE LEADERSHIP FACTOR MESH

Leader Style	Catalyst	Commander	Encourager	Hermit
Follower Style	Participant	Dependent	Receiver	Self-Starter
Ministry Situation	Cooperative	Unstable-Overstable	Orderly	Self-Sustaining

style to the particular demands of followers and ministry situations is called "style flex."[9] Adjusting styles is usually done by the leader because he has the freedom to select his own style and to help structure ministry situations. In other words, the leader has leverage over two of the three elements of leadership mesh.

It's instructive to note how flexibly Jesus applied leader styles. He was a Catalyst primarily; the raising of Lazarus (John 11:43; 12:9-11), the mass feedings (Mark 6:34-44; 8:1-9), and the wedding feast at Cana (John 2:1-11) demonstrate some key catalytic events. Jesus illustrated Commander tendencies in several short-term situations such as cleansing the Temple (John 2:16; Mark 11:15) and in some of his miracles (John 5:8; Mark 1:27; 4:39). Jesus the Encourager is shown in the high priestly prayer (John 17) and in the comfort he offered others (John 4:50; 14:1; Mark 14:8). Occasionally, Jesus used the Hermit approach and retreated to refurbish his body and soul (Mark 6:32, 46; John 7:10). He masterfully matched his style to the demands of his ministry.

Who Initiates Style Flex?

What happens when the leader and follower styles are obviously out of sync? Who should "give" and make adjustments? My suggestion is that the leader shift his approach as much as he can in good conscience for as long as needed. One person has more flexibility than a group.

When Do You Use Style Flex?

A catalog of style flex timing factors helps leaders analyze the leadership situations they face for possible style flex occasions.

Catalysts minister effectively when . . .

- Adequate resources are at hand.
- A team of mature, trained workers is present.
- Enough time and patience are available.
- Mass involvement is indicated.
- The congregation is heterogeneous and pluralistic.
- Long-range goals are at stake.

Commanders function best when . . .
- Confusion and chaos reign.
- Dependent personalities make up the group.
- Inertia has taken over the congregation.
- Quick responses and short-term results are preferred.

Encouragers work well when . . .
- Relational issues and fellowship are paramount.
- An emotional change of pace is needed.
- Healing is needed by individuals or by the congregation.

Hermits are called for when . . .
- Rest and recreation are needed by the leader or by the congregation at large.
- A moratorium is necessary to let emotions in the congregation lessen.
- Time is required to discover better decision-making options.

Usually, I'm asked at this point if a leader can switch to other styles occasionally and still keep his integrity. I think so—if several conditions prevail. (1) The leader has identified and understands his preferred style. (2) He realizes what he has been attempting isn't good for the congregation or for members' morale. (3) He knows that he's making a temporary adjustment, and he understands why a short-term change is apt to be more effective than his usual style. (4) He's comfortable with his motives. (5) In some instances, he may choose to tell his followers what he's trying to do and why.

Here's an example of style flex. A pastor friend is an extremely effective Catalyst. He accepted a new pastorate in a congregation with a history of conflict. When he entered the congregation, it was weary of fighting and inert. After sizing up the overall situation, this pastor met with his lay leaders and proposed a plan. He tenderly described the stagnation he saw in the congregation. Further, he explained how crucial he felt it was to regain some momentum for the mission goals the group had identified with him in a joint process. "For six months," he said, "I'd like to take command and get us moving toward the three goals we've chosen. Then, I'd like to move into my more natural style and work as a player-coach to help us develop leaders, programs, and processes for our long-term ministry."

At this point he fell silent to hear the group's response. One member quickly stood and spoke what turned out to be the group's sentiment. "Hallelujah," he exuded, "I've been a deacon in this church for twenty-five years, and this is the first time I've ever known what the game plan is!"

Which Style Flex Adjustments Are Easiest to Make?

A number of factors figure into the ease of style flexing. In general, the simplest style flex changes to make are . . .

- from the more active and balanced to the more passive and tilted styles;
- from the more flexible to the more rigid styles;
- from the longer term to the more temporary styles;
- from the less radical switches in behavior to the greater changes.

Leadership Under Pressure

Most of us have a dominant, preferred leader style and a backup style we automatically switch to in emergencies.[10] Our so-called backup style may differ from our deliberate style. We switch to our backup approach unconsciously when triggered emotionally, unconsciously, and without calculation.

I suspect our backup styles are reversions to more primitive behaviors. They reveal our less civilized selves. When the caveman found himself face-to-face with a saber-toothed tiger in some prehistoric jungle clearing, the options were few and transparent —fight to the death or run for his life. The tendency of cornered leaders is similar: charge or retreat.

I've noticed how my own backup style works. When all's well, I try to be a Catalyst—fair, balanced, participative. When someone goes for my jugular, my response instantly takes a radical turn. I switch to the Commander stance—confrontational, demanding, authoritarian. Like Teddy Roosevelt, I charge up the San Juan hills of life directly at my perceived adversary. *By George,* I tell myself, *I'm going to get this job done or issue settled right now no matter what it takes.* In my most extreme Commander state, I take no prisoners. In fact, I may occasionally adopt a kamikaze approach and go all out to defeat my "enemy."

This Dr. Jekyll and Mr. Hyde change surprises me at times and usually catches my followers off guard too. They generally have seen me as easygoing and evenhanded. Then when I'm threatened and my adrenalin begins to pump, they all see another side of the "good ol' boy."

Here's one way to get a clue to your backup style. Watch your own behavior when you're pressured at home or in private settings. How you react in these circumstances may help you monitor and guard against public leadership situations where you're apt to lose your cool and overreact.

I help my students get a glimpse of their backup style by creating a laboratory in the classroom. I use a learning game to create competitive, leaderless groups. Two teams are pitted against each other. Short time frames are set, and the seconds left in each round are called out regularly. Team scores are announced at the end of every round. In other words, a lot of pressure is put on the participants. They react in fascinating ways. Some folks take charge, others follow enthusiastically, and a few withdraw completely. Some take risks, others calculate and play it safe. What seems to emerge in these experiences is a taste of their backup style. That's an important piece of information for any leader.

Leader styles, follower styles, ministry situations—all call for effective match ups. The foundation for meshing styles, however, is a clear leader style selection.

Style Is a Choice

Life is a series of choices—some of them very tough. A character in *The Teahouse of the August Moon* says life doesn't consist of the big decisions without answers or the small decisions with automatic answers. Rather, he claims, life is the living of the middle-sized question. For those who attempt to lead volunteers in the church, one of the middle-sized questions is selecting leader styles that work. It's one of our tougher choices.

Have You Chosen?

I couldn't believe my ears. My two friends weren't saying anything heretical, but their ideas were unfamiliar to me. Eavesdrop with me.

YOUNG MINISTER: "I can't get the members of my congregation to follow me. I try my best. But nothing really happens. What can I do?"

OLDER MINISTER: "What have you tried?"

YOUNGER MINISTER: "Everything I know to do. I've begged and threatened and quoted Scripture and thrown up my hands in despair. What's left?"

OLDER MINISTER: "Let me suggest several experiments. Try this for a week or two. Give orders. Tell them what to do, when to do it, and what will happen if they don't respond. Set goals and deadlines. Hold their feet to the fire. At the end of this experimental period, add up the results. What was accomplished? How did the people respond? How do you feel about what happened? How do you feel about yourself?"

My young friend gulped when he considered the trial which had just been suggested. "OK," he said slowly. "Then what?"

OLDER MINISTER: "Next try doing nothing at all. Hide. Retreat. Make no suggestions and take no initiatives. Just fold your hands and wait out your experimental period. Then ask yourself the same set of questions I mentioned after the first experiment."

YOUNGER MINISTER: with a doubtful tone: "Well, I guess I could try that too. Then what?"

OLDER MINISTER: "For a set time frame, call for broad-based partici-

pation. Share ideas. Listen closely to others' suggestions. Help
the group develop their plans and make their own decisions.
Use the same questions as before to evaluate your results."

They discussed various approaches on how to "try on and try out"
these style options. And then I heard the conclusion of the experiment: "After you've tasted a range of leader styles and know
what's comfortable for you and your members, make a choice.
Choose the leader style that's authentic and works best for you in
your congregation. Then use it consistently."

While I wasn't willing to experiment on my congregation in the
fashion suggested, I couldn't get the concept of choosing my style
out of my mind. I could choose my own leader style! The idea was
fresh and powerful for me. *Why was the idea new?* I wondered. I had
never before really thought about how my approach to ministry
could be adjusted by a deliberate choice.

Then, I realized something I'd never seen before. I'd grown up
in one church and had only seen one leadership style used. My
boyhood pastors had tried to lead that rural church in the Missouri
mountains with a "prophetic" approach. Every Sunday they
would preach themselves to the brink of cardiac arrest with demand after demand. With an exception or two, they soon faced
counterdemands from the congregation. Their prophetic styles
wore thin after a while. I had seen the results of their patterns but
had never realized there were other style options available to me.

You can choose your leader style! That's good news. Choosing
your leadership style is not the same as choosing to be a leader,
however. Folks who are selected and placed in positions of influence in their congregations are leaders—like it or not, effective or
not. But you can decide how you'll exercise your leadership action
as a pattern—that's your leader style. It's also the beginning point
of a production leader-follower-situation match.

Notes

1 I've explored the leader-follower-situation mesh in "Leader Style and Church Staff Mesh," *Review and Expositor* 78 (Winter 1981), pp. 15-27.

2 For applied situational perspectives on followership, see Joseph A Steger, George E. Manners, Jr., and Thomas W. Zimmerer, "Following the Leader: How To Link Management Style to Subordinate Personalities," *Management Review*, Oct. 1982, pp. 22-28, 49-51; Jerry H. Edmondson, "The Director of Missions and Situational Leadership," *Associational Bulletin*, Sept. 1982, pp. 1-2; "Try Matching the Behavioral Styles of Managers and Support Staff," *Training/HRD*, Feb. 1978, pp. 14-15; and Dewey A. Yeager, "Understanding—and Adapting—Your Instructional Style," *Training/HRD*, Dec. 1981, pp. 44, 48.

3 Attributed to Oscar Romo in Dan Martin's article, "The Church-Growth Questions," *Home Missions*, Dec. 1977, p. 12.

4 Maria Carmen Gear, Ernesto Cesar Liendo, and Lila Lee Scott, *Patients and Agents: Transference-Countertransference in Therapy* (New York: Jason Aronson, 1983), pp. 22-44.

5 Quoted in Albert Camus, *The Rebel: An Essay on Man in Revolt* (Revised and translated by Anthony Bower (New York: Vintage Books, 1958), p. 251.

6 Gear, *Patients and Agents*, pp. 45-73.

7 For perspectives on structure in work situations, see Daniel A. Tagliere *People, Power, and Organization* (New York: Amacom, 1973), pp. 25-58; Raymond A. Gumpert and Ronald K. Hambleton, "Situational Leadership," *Management Review*, Dec. 1979, pp. 8-12; R. Jeffery Ellis, "Organizational Leadership in Turbulent Times," *Management Review*, Mar. 1983, pp. 59-61; and Fred E. Fiedler and Martin M. Chemers, *Improving Leadership Effectiveness: The Leader Match Concept* (New York: John Wiley and Sons, 1976), pp. 152-158.

8 Fiedler and Chemers, *Improving Leadership Effectiveness*. p. 136.

9 Ron Zemke, "Better Ways to Help Train People," *Training/HRD*, Aug. 1976, pp. 12-16.

10 Robert R. Blake and Jane S. Mouton, *The New Managerial Grid* (Houston: Gulf Publishing, 1978), p. 205; Jane Srygley Mouton and Robert R. Blake, *The Marriage Grid* (New York: McGraw-Hill, 1971), pp. 15-17,53,61-62.

5
Your Leader Style and People

He spoke apologetically. I was leading a conflict management conference in Mississippi when a middle-aged participant approached me at the end of the first session. "I'm new in the ministry. I'm so far behind all of these other ministers that I don't belong here."

"What has your work been until now?" I inquired.

"I've owned a retail hardware store for thirty years," he answered.

After further conversation, I discovered he had been a highly successful merchant and a longtime lay leader working actively in his church.

"You're probably ahead of the pack," I observed. "Nobody operates a neighborhood business successfully for an extended period of time without good people skills and management abilities. You've had some rich experiences in and beyond the church. You probably can do things relationally that some pastors never learn."

He participated in the remainder of the seminar with more confidence. He seemed to sense that he had something to offer the group after all. He could relate to people. John D. Rockefeller, Sr., asserted, "I will pay more for the ability to deal with people than any other ability under the sun." Probably the most crucial ability any ministry leader offers his congregation is getting along with people.

The Value of People

People are valuable. Created in God's image and recreated by the life and death of Christ—that means we're worthwhile. In fact, the value we place on persons provides the foundation for our relationships. If I don't see myself as valuable, I don't offer myself to others. I have nothing to give to them. If I don't see others as of value, I don't make the effort to get to know them. After all, I can receive nothing from a relationship with them. The bottom line is: effective leaders value themselves and others and behave accordingly.

One biblical word for the church as community is *koinonia*. We build a lot of our "people" words and phrases on the ideas spinning off koinonia: partner; companion; in common; bound together; shares with; fellowship. Congregations are people, not places. We are together with Christ and with each other. We're a community of faith, action, and interaction.

Religious communities have traditionally demonstrated their values by making covenants. We live together in the church by our promises to each other; they are the ties that bind us into community. Covenants may be entered into by unequals—our commitments with and to God, for instance. However, convenants between equals form the glue for the human grouping we call church. What do covenants provide to congregations?

- Covenants make relationships between people dependable.
- Covenants clarify our values and priorities.
- Covenants establish a basis for evaluating our relationships.
- Covenants provide us a foundation for renewing our relationships.

Relational Bridges for Leadership

Relationships between persons provide both beginning points

and bridges for ministry. Ministry happens person-to-person. So we build and maintain relationships so quality ministry can occur.

Relationships require an initiator. Someone has to make the first move and break the ice. Ministry leaders take the risks involved in initiative. It goes with the territory.

Both Catalysts and Commanders are people approachers. They can take initiative. The Catalyst involves people to help them grow and the congregation to move forward. The Commander favors production interests and may develop relationships to provide manpower for his goals.

Encouragers and Hermits don't initiate relationships as readily. The Encourager is somewhat more apt to let others set the relational agenda and take the first steps in relating. Hermits are unsure about relationships, and if shy find taking initiative uncomfortable.

Relationships also require cultivation. Friendships don't grow automatically. They need nurture and maintenance. Someone must tend relationships or they atrophy.

Catalysts, Commanders, and Encouragers maintain established relationships well. The Catalyst believes in people and cultivates their participation. The Commander needs folks to help him achieve his selected tasks. The Encourager likes people and invests lots of time in socializing. The Hermit may not relate to lots of people but may still develop a few close contacts.

Consequences of Leaders' "People Patterns"

Over time each of us develops a fairly predictable manner of relating to others. We become comfortable in dealing with people in a certain way. Therefore, our leader style and our "people patterns" of relational preferences mesh to a significant extent.[1] Again, allow me to overstate the case at times to draw the comparisons and contrasts more starkly.

Catalysts: Assertive with People

Assertive leaders respect others and like themselves. They can and do stand up for their own needs without abusing or dominating others. Assertive folks value themselves and affirm the worth of others simultaneously. Because of this balance, there really isn't overassertive behavior.

What are the advantages of assertive behavior?

- Assertiveness indicates a measure of healthy self-esteem. In his Great Commandment, Jesus instructed us to love ourselves as a model for loving others (Matt. 22:39).
- Assertiveness fosters fulfilling relationships.
- Assertiveness reduces fears of being abused or controlled.
- Assertiveness helps you live your own life, meet your goals, and promote your values fairly. Even when assertive behavior doesn't work for you, you still can take comfort in having lived by the Golden Rule. You've treated others with the same consideration you expect from them (Matt. 7:12).

Assertiveness also contains some risks.

- Assertive relating may call for learning new behaviors, especially if your habit has been either to submit to or to dominate others.
- Assertive behavior may make you feel confrontational at times even though it's attempted caringly and honestly. We may feel uneasy and vulnerable when we identify our own self-interests.
- Assertiveness may lead to conflict. When you're relating to folk who are used to getting their own way, assertive behavior may appear threateningly abrasive to them.
- Assertiveness forces you to clarify your identity, personal values, and goals. That's both hard work and an ongoing task.

Catalysts tend to be assertive leaders. They view themselves and others positively. Catalysts are people involvers. Their participative style lends itself to assertiveness.

Commanders: Aggressive with People

Aggressive literally means "to move against." That is, aggressive people tend to express their feelings, needs, and ideas at others' expense. They want the last word, argue to win, and try to dominate relationally. In their most pronounced form, they "squeeze other men as if they were oranges."[2] Aggressive people carry chips on their shoulders.

Does aggressive behavior have benefits?

- Aggressors often get what they want. They overpower others and make their goals the group's goals.
- Aggressive people are good at protecting themselves, lessening personal vulnerability, and competing well.
- Aggressors control others. Others frequently do what aggressors demand.

Are there disadvantages to aggressiveness?

- Some aggressives push their point of view because they really feel weak. Of course, their behavior tends to make enemies for them. So, the end result of their aggressiveness is increased fearfulness.
- "Uneasy rests the head that wears the crown" applies especially to aggressors. Authoritarian behavior creates opposition and contains the seeds of its own destruction. The Old Testament Book of Esther describes the aggressive Persian official Haman. Killing Mordecai was Haman's chief goal in life, although Mordecai's only "sin" was that he didn't grovel before Haman. A gallows was built at Haman's order for the execution of Mordecai. However, Haman's overaggressiveness led to his downfall. In the end "they hanged Haman on the gallows which he had prepared for Mordecai" (Esther 7:10).
- Aggressive behavior may result, paradoxically, in loss of control. Few people like to be dominated; they look for

ways to "beat the system." Any tactic which vetoes the power of the aggressor may be employed.

- In quiet moments, the aggressor may feel guilty about his overbearing actions.
- Aggressors use people and treat them as objects rather than fellow pilgrims.
- Aggressors create a double bind for themselves. They don't respect underlings and can't develop peer relationships. They end up lonely.

Commanders are apt to be aggressive. Since they downplay the place of others' needs and feelings, Commanders lean toward an autocratic leader style. Relationally, these leaders wear their welcomes out fairly soon—in spite of being productive in other ministry areas.

Encouragers: Submissive with People

Submissives place their own rights and needs on the back burner and allow others to take the relational initiative. These behaviors reduce the submissive's impact on others. Their submissiveness undercuts being taken seriously. Submissives sometimes feel fragile and, therefore, see others as too fragile to interact with or to confront. Even if they express their needs, they present themselves apologetically or qualify their feelings. In their extreme form, submissives let others ignore them and deny their rights.

Up to 80 percent of Americans claim they act in a submissive fashion. We're either a nation of nice guys or one of willing victims. In the same spirit, many churches operate on a norm of niceness. In these genteel congregations, the most offensive sin is to be "not nice." Ungentlemanly or unladylike behavior is worse than un-Christian acts.

Submissive behavior has its payoffs.

- Submissives get praised as selfless. They're good sports. They go the second mile. These pleasant, easygoing submissives are prime candidates for the "good ol' boy" network.

- Submissives avoid conflict—or at least try to avoid it.
- Submission is culturally endorsed. We're trained to be "good little boys" and "nice little girls" and to submit to parents, teachers, and other authorities.
- Submissives escape responsibility. They keep a low profile. When things go wrong, they deflect blame by claiming they were "just doing their job."
- Submissive behavior invites others to help you. Others are enticed to rescue the helpless person.
- Ironically, submissives can end up controlling others. For example, the threat of a woman's tears has often controlled a man's response.
  Niceness has its prices too.
- The submissive person allows others to direct his life. God's unique plan for his life goes unfulfilled.
- Deep and durable relationships aren't fully developed by submissives. They bend to others' definitions of love, meet others' expectations, and settle for shallow relationships. As the Bible points out, we can conquer the whole world but still forfeit our own best selves (Matt. 16:26).
- Submissives surrender half of their emotions. They show the positive emotions of love and joy but repress emotions they interpret as negative. Anger and related feelings are considered too threatening and are either swallowed or diverted.

Encouragers lean toward submissive behaviors. They are so sensitive to others and their concerns that they allow their own needs and organizational issues to recede into the background. Encouragers tend to let others set the interpersonal agenda.

Hermit: Nonassertive with People

Nonassertives try to stay uninvolved. They attempt relational neutrality. Nonassertives choose to take no initiative and no risks toward others. They don't value themselves or others sufficiently to approach people comfortably.

Are there pluses in nonassertive behavior?

- Nonassertives practice safety first. They use nonassertion as a survival tactic and make self-preservation their main goal.
- Nonassertion reduces the odds of rejection. Nothing is risked; therefore, nothing is lost.

What are the minuses of nonassertion?

- Nonassertives deprive their congregations of their potential contribution.
- Tragically, in a few cases, nonassertive behavior doesn't even allow this type to defend himself. Extreme nonassertion virtually invites abuse.

Hermits tend toward nonassertion. They aren't comfortable with others and apparently don't believe in themselves. Relationally, Hermits tie their own hands.

When Groups Turn into Cliques

Ministry leaders must relate to groups as well as individuals. That's because we're rarely satisfied to maintain only one-to-one relationships. We humans are so social we tend to form groups.[3] Families, committees, and study classes are natural groupings for congregations.

Sometimes, though, being "in" with the in crowd doesn't seem to be enough. We want more status or prestige or power than simply belonging gives. Then we begin a perverse process. We draw the lines of group identification more visibly and define our "in-ness" by others' "outness." Our group becomes our clique, closed off from others to identify or protect us.

Cliques demand other "out" persons or groups. That is, our clique must provide something special, something the "outs" can't or won't give us. Then it becomes easy to draw the contrasts that make "us" special and "them" common. Right and wrong. Good and bad. Young and old. Male and female. Local and national. We use these kinds of polarities to define our group's uniqueness.

The Pharisees of the New Testament illustrate a noble group which became a clique. They began as a model group, a pattern of pure living. They deteriorated into a rigid, legalistic clique. By Jesus' time, the Pharisees called themselves "the separated ones" and took as much pride in being superior as in being orthodox. They looked down on common folks who couldn't live up to their standards. The end result? They made themselves judge and jury of the morals of the masses. Jesus called them hypocrites and well-groomed tombs (Matt. 23:27-28).

Cliques are outgrowths of the informal "people" side of congregations, not the formal "goal" side. That is, most organizations exist to get work done; they live for their mission. But the people who work toward that mission have needs beyond the mission itself. For instance, they have needs to know beyond the information shared through newsletters and on bulletin boards—so a "grapevine" emerges to "put the word out." They have a need to feel secure—so an "underground" develops to "protect our interests." The informal organization is natural to all congregations. Effective ministry leaders tap into and cultivate the grapevine, the informal communications channels. They take seriously the human need for security so that underground movements aren't as necessary.

Catalysts recognize that special groups emerge in almost any congregation and work to reconnect them to the larger body. They keep decision making and change processes open and slow moving enough to encourage broad participation. Catalyst leaders prevent some cliques from forming because of their participative approach. They also keep established cliques from moving further away from the mainstream of the congregation into an isolated orbit.

Commanders inadvertently encourage cliques to form by their dominating styles. They "divide the house" into groups who are "for me" or "against me." Then they define congregational issues in moral terms—constructive and destructive, traditional and radical, and true and false. Commanders create closed systems and stress control mechanisms which entrench cliques more deeply. At times, Commanders make an enemy out of all outsiders and turn their congregation into one large clique.

Encouragers generally relate well with groups and go out of their way to work with cliques' diverse interpersonal needs. Encouragers are vulnerable, however, when a production-oriented clique of young turks insists that the congregation as a whole move forward. Task demands may put the Encourager in retreat.

Hermits' passivity gives tacit approval to cliques. When there's a leadership vacuum in a congregation, it's every man for himself. Cliques develop around special interests and lobbying begins. The Hermit pulls back farther and the wrestling for control of the congregational agenda continues unabated. The congregational atmosphere becomes polarized and politicized.

Church Leader as Politician

At first his statement surprised me and offended me a bit. Politics in the church? He said, "After twenty-five years as a pastor, I've finally admitted there's a political dimension to ministry in a congregation." Now I think he was right.

Ministry inevitably contains an element of politics. Why? Because congregations are interdependent webs of different personalities and varied goals. People working with people yields a political atmosphere.

Traditionally, two basic secular sources have provided ministers some helpful perspectives on leadership: business management and political science. The congregational leader's role is more akin to the politician than the businessman in several important ways. Both ministers and politicians relate to varied constituencies. Both feel the impact of the shifting tides of trust and mistrust. Both are confronted by the "What have you done for me lately?" attitude. Both can be tempted to become manipulators. And both may lose their sense of humor.

Humor: Keeping Life in Perspective

In the biblically flavored play *Lazarus Laughed,* Lazarus, now alive again, is asked how it feels to die. In response Lazarus laughs and replies, "There is no death." Is it appropriate to laugh and speak of death simultaneously? Certainly.

Humor puts perspective, proportion, and seasoning into our lives. When we can't do much about our circumstances, a belly laugh or at least a chuckle may put life's pieces back together enough so that we can move on. Theologically speaking, humor is one way we identify the disjunctions between our ideals and our realities. A sense of our own sinfulness balances us enough to realize we can't afford to take ourselves too seriously.

Christ had a sense of humor, contrary to some popular perceptions. It was rooted in the contrast between childlikeness and maturity. This contrast lends perspective.

Elton Trueblood observes:

> The balance between the childlike and the mature in Christ's life is really amazing. . . . On the one hand, He can rejoice unconditionally in the Father's care, without which not a sparrow falls, but, on the other hand, He can see through the pretensions of men and women, particularly their religious pretensions. Because, in Christ, there was the acme of both the childlike and the mature, humor was inevitable. Humor appears where the two worlds meet.[4]

One way to recognize the leader styles of ourselves and others is to analyze the leader's use of humor. Catalysts, for example, fit humor to the situation. The incongruities of an incident overflow spontaneously in the Catalyst's conversation. His sense of humor tends to be philosophical and realistic. Furthermore, he sees and notes life's big and little ironies. Sometimes the Catalyst uses humor in a gently self-deprecating manner. That is, he can poke fun at himself but won't belittle others.

The Commander tends to use humor as a control mechanism. He may use humor as a tool to sell himself. Or he may use humor comparatively. That is, the Commander may slip a put-down into his conversation. You can feel the bite and hear the too-loud, harsh-edged gallows laugh.

Tragically, some Commanders are essentially humorless. Several years ago I watched a television interview of a presidential candidate. At the end of the conversation, the interviewer caught the candidate flat-footed. "Governor," he said, "tell me your favorite joke." The candidate, never at a loss for words before, looked blank and stammered aimlessly for several moments. Then the candidate gathered himself a bit and replied, "I don't know any jokes."

In that instant, I knew intuitively that I couldn't vote for that candidate. It wasn't that he knew no funny stories. His whole reaction—expression, body language, and verbal answer—conveyed a complete lack of humor. When I compared his humorlessness with his tough rhetoric on political issues, I questioned his ability to keep political decisions in perspective. In short, his humorlessness frightened me a bit. I guess I'm constitutionally suspicious of humorless leaders. At least, I prefer my supervisors to have a good sense of perspective since I'm not perfect, and neither are they.

Some Encouragers have a joke for every occasion. They're the life of the party and easy to listen to when they're on the stump. They are masters of using the funny anecdote to ease tension and shift attention away from controversy. They communicate well because they use humor to change the emotional pace of what they're saying. Encouragers seem to have an innate sense that humor is a "social lubricant" as the comedian Steve Allen describes it.

Hermits don't display a public sense of humor too often. However, many of them show a good sense of humor in private conversation. A Hermit friend of mine writes biting satire. I wonder if he doesn't wish he could show his wit more comfortably in group settings. In lieu of public expressions of humor, he confines himself to nipping at people and issues behind the scenes only.

As I Was Saying

The patterns congregational leaders develop in relating to people is one of the acid tests of leadership. After all, churches are only people.

Notes

1 This segment of material draws heavily on Robert Bolton, *People Skills* (Englewood Cliffs: Prentice-Hall, 1979), pp. 123-138.

2 Ibid., p. 125.

3 For perspectives on cliques, see James H. Davis, *Group Performance* (Reading, MA: Addison-Wesley, 1969), pp. 71-87; Kurt Lewin, *Resolving Social Conflicts* (New York: Harper, 1948); and Clyde Reid, *Groups Alive, Church Alive* (New York: Harper and Row, 1969), pp. 61-75.

4 Elton Trueblood, *The Humor of Christ* (New York: Harper and Row, 1964), p. 39.

6
Your Leader Style and Craftsmanship

Leadership is both an art and a craft. An art—the personal touch, accurate intuition, a sense of timing. Those arts really can't be taught. A craft—a range of skills, a variety of abilities, a set of capabilities. Craftsmanship can be developed to a significant extent.

The signs of craftsmanship show through. Here's a striking example of skill honed to a masterful level.[1] Legendary golfer Ben Hogan hit a one-iron to the 72nd green in the 1950 US Open. A photo of this shot appeared in *Life* magazine and became famous in the annals of American golf. Somewhere between the shot and Hogan's arrival on the green, an overzealous fan stole the one-iron out of Hogan's bag. For thirty-three years the club remained missing.

Recently, however, the one-iron was found by a Raleigh, North Carolina, man and returned to a grateful Hogan. Jackie Murdock, a dealer in classic clubs, bought a set of old clubs with the one-iron missing. The man Murdock purchased the clubs from gave him a one-iron, but it didn't match the rest of the set after all. Murdock was intrigued by a rumor passed along by the former owner of the one-iron that Hogan had used it in the 1950 US Open. An interesting story, Murdock thought, but highly unlikely.

But a close examination of the old one-iron stimulated Murdock's curiosity. There was a worn area, an indentation about the size of a quarter, exactly on the iron's sweet spot. The original owner of this club had been a craftsman, a master who could hit the ball in the same place on the club face time after time.

Murdock showed the one-iron to his college friend, pro golfer Lanny Wadkins. Wadkins volunteered to take the club back home to Texas with him and let Hogan examine it. Shortly after, Murdock received this letter from Hogan:

> Dear Mr. Murdock:
> Just a note to thank you for allowing me to see and possess my old No. 1 iron. I likened this to the return of an old, long-lost friend.
> > Sincerely,
> > Ben Hogan

So the story moved full cycle—all because Hogan could hit a golf ball more precisely than anyone else. The identation was Hogan's trademark, the sign of his craftsmanship. To indicate how phenomenal Hogan's precision was, Arnold Palmer claims the difference between an absolutely straight golf shot and the one that veers off course is a swing variance of only .004 of an inch! That requires the highest degree of craftsmanship.

Let's explore a sample array of congregational leader skills. Craftsmanship or the use of skills relates to leader styles also.

Planning: the Craft of Envisioning

One of the characters in the film *Paint Your Wagon* surmises that he was born under a wandering star. He divides the wanderers of the world into two types: ones who are going somewhere and those going nowhere. His point is well taken. Everybody and everything changes. But if a choice can be made, going some specific somewhere is to be preferred.

A mutual mission gives a congregation identity and direction.[2] Healthy churches work from a visionary foundation and toward an ultimate vision. In other words, a ministry dream provides a church both an anchor and sails. For instance, Thomas A. Edison set a goal—the completion of a major invention every six months and a minor invention every ten days. Propelled by his dream,

Edison developed nearly half of his 1,093 patents in the eight year span between 1876 and 1884. His goal provided both a launch pad and a target for Edison.

After a congregation has clarified its unique personality and defined its fundamental reason for being, it can develop a change process to bring its dream into reality. Four steps can guide congregational changes.

1. Raising congregational consciousness. An "aha" experience of organizational need makes change legitimate. Such an experience is often like a seed slowly sprouting, growing, then budding, finally bursting into full bloom. These experiences feel sudden, but in congregational settings a lot of talking and listening and researching and teaching usually preceded switching the light bulbs on in members' heads.

2. Broadening decision-making information. A forum approach to congregational decision making provides discussion sessions before and apart from actually deciding. Two advantages flow out of this approach. The information gathering and sharing processes enjoy broad participation. And the immediate pressure is taken off the event of deciding.

3. Empowering others for ministry. The confidence which emerges out of a keen sense of need and a wider knowledge of the facts helps members feel they can deal with change successfully. They feel they have some handles on the problem.

4. Implementing action plans. The old saw goes: plan your work and work your plan. There's a bit more to implementation of change than that. Some suggestions? Implement change in manageable increments. Allow the congregation to adjust and regain its sense of equilibrium after each change effort. Celebrate your successful changes and make them standard operating procedure.

Catalysts build congregational unity around a mutually developed vision. They take seriously the diverse interests and the varied backgrounds of members. Using participative processes, they develop congregational plans around the core mission of the group.

Catalysts realize that some folks petrify and resist change. Balladeer Arlo Guthrie conveys much sensitivity in his concerts. Recently he ended a show by singing the old hymn "Amazing Grace." He told about the song's composer, John Newton, former slave ship captain who turned around in midtrip and took his final load of passengers back to Africa. Guthrie's conclusion? "Anybody who's not afraid to turn around is a friend of mine."[3]

Catalysts take a lot of the threat out of change by helping members define the central mission of their church first. Healthy organizations can and do change according to their visions.

Commanders often define congregational vision primarily by their own interests. They major on production goals and tilt toward an investment in organizational change efforts.

Encouragers major on personal change issues in their members' lives. Their preference for relational change can leave organizational direction setting for others to do.

Hermits remain too detached from organizational concerns to create much change. Even the changes they prefer may not be possible because they have such a poor relational base.

Communication: the Craft of Clarifying

Clear communication aids effective leadership. But good communication isn't automatic. A newspaper columnist friend claims she's in a constant search for the perfect sentence. According to her, that elusive sentence is clean with an unmistakable meaning.

Remember the crisp answer Willie Sutton, the bank robber, gave to a reporter's question "Why did you rob banks?" Sutton replied, "That's where the money was!" In spite of Sutton's ethics, he was an excellent communicator.

Sending a message clearly by speaking or writing is only one side of communication. Sending information only puts the intended message into code. The other side of communication, the decoding dimension, calls for careful listening and sensitive feedback.

Listening is such hard work that its intense concentration even causes our blood pressure to rise slightly. Listening ranges across three levels of interaction. First, we listen for facts. This process involves skimming off and isolating key ideas, outlining presentations or chapters, and summarizing perspectives.

Second, we listen with our hearts for others' feelings. How things are said has as much impact as what is said. George White-field, the famous colonial evangelist, "could make men laugh or cry by pronouncing the word 'Mesopotamia' ".

Third, we train ourselves to listen with our eyes. The nonverbals of body language and the atmosphere of places communicate many messages crucial to effective ministry. Embodying communication is basic to the Christian gospel. After all, the incarnation of Christ reminds us that God's revelation became a living Word to communicate with us (John 1:14).

Communication in congregational contexts is also important to leaders. I've already mentioned the grapevine, an organization's informal communication network. To the surprise of many, the grapevine carries mostly accurate information, not just casual gossip. Grapevines' questionable reputation in some quarters grows out of their tendency when they are inaccurate to overstate, distort, and spread rumors.[4] Mark Twain made the point well: "A lie can travel around the world while the truth is putting on its shoes."

Formal communication channels are indigenous to organized life. For example, family leaders transmit religious and historic foundations to their clans. "What do these stones mean?" the Hebrew youngsters asked their fathers (Josh. 4:6,21). Then the stories of faith were recounted. In congregational settings, the official storytellers describe the church's dream, convey its values, lionize its heroes, and lend continuity to its ongoing ministries.

Catalysts help congregations choose and publicize the directions of their ministries. They speak, listen, and give feedback on request.

Commanders are primarily tellers. They generally communicate well. But they neglect to listen and share feedback.

Encouragers listen well and sometimes make their concerns clearly known. They are careful to clarify misunderstandings and work hard to link up diverse interests within the congregation.

Hermits' isolation makes effective communication difficult. They are more apt to listen than to speak up. When they give their point of view, they prefer selective, private settings rather than general, public ones.

Motivation: the Craft of Energizing

"History has been written not by the most talented but by the most motivated" is management expert Peter Drucker's estimate. He's probably right. Harry Truman agreed with Drucker. Truman claimed that the world is run by *C* students. I'd add that the *C* students who end up in charge of significant efforts are clearly focused on their goals. They're motivated, in other words.

Self-motivation grows out of a sense of identity and direction. Knowing who you are and where you're headed is a powerful force. Connie Mack, the late professional baseball manager, observed,

> I've seen boys on my baseball team go into slumps and never come out of them, and I've seen others snap right out and come back better than ever. I guess more players lick themselves than are ever licked by an opposing team. The first thing a man has to know is how to handle himself.

Typically, even apathetic congregations have at least a few pockets of enthusiasm in them. These energy reservoirs are invaluable resources; they signal that golden quality called motivation. Churches have members who are committed to their special interests—singing in the choir, teaching Sunday School, reaching out to the unchurched, or ministering to the aged. These energy reservoirs must be nurtured and channeled toward the congregation's major goals.

How can members' energies be guided into ministry efforts?[5]

● Take members' needs seriously. Abraham Maslow described

humans as "ever-wanting" creatures. People will work to meet real needs—theirs and others.

• Eliminate irritants from the congregational climate. Dissatisfiers in the church's environment are barriers to motivation. These dissatisfiers create an uphill, rowing-against-the-tide feeling and must be overcome before people will invest their energies in ministry.

• Create a climate in which members can serve Christ naturally. Show appreciation. Develop teamwork. Secure clear agreements for work to be done. These are a few leader actions which leaven the congregational climate positively.

Catalysts believe people are intrinsically motivated. Theologically speaking, they hold that the Holy Spirit energizes Christians, and, therefore, Catalysts help their members discover and use their gifts in service. They develop structures to allow the full range of members' motivations to be expressed.

Commanders belong to the "swift-kick-in-the-pants" school of motivation. They press their members to follow orders at any expense. Motivation for them is mainly external. Commanders could learn an important lesson on leadership from General Eisenhower. He would take a piece of string, place it on a table, and demonstrate a crucial contrast for leaders. Pull the string, and it will follow. Push the string, and it balls up and goes nowhere at all.

Encouragers belong to the rah-rah school of motivation. They urge others to grow and serve. Encouragers believe in the abilities of their members. They aren't always as good, however, at pointing toward goals which deserve the motivational energies of those members.

Hermits feel apathetic and unmotivated toward concerns beyond their own survival. They are unsure enough of others to doubt that anyone really has much energy for service.

Supervision: the Craft of Supporting

Ordinarily, I don't enjoy being a guinea pig, but this experience proved interesting. I had gone to the teaching clinic at Vanderbilt Medical School for an eye examination. An ophthalmologist entered the examining room, greeted me, and introduced me to a young medical student on his first day of residency in the eye clinic. I quickly realized two facts: I was the specimen, and I would become an interested observer of the examination.

The teacher physician would describe in detail to the student physician what he was preparing to do to me and why. Then the ophthalmologist would examine my eyes. Finally, it was the student's turn. "What do you see?" he'd ask the student. The young resident would peer into my eyes and describe what he saw in somewhat uncertain terms. "Good, good," the ophthalmologist would usually reply. Both the student and I would then silently sigh with relief. Occasionally, the ophthalmologist would instruct, "See that? That's normal. If the eye was diseased, you'd see . . ." and he'd describe the difference in detail.

Finally, we reached my least favorite part of an eye exam— dilating the pupil. The ophthalmologist turned to the student. "I'm going to place drops in his eyes to dilate them. Will his pupils become larger or smaller?" My anxiety increased considerably when the student guessed the wrong response. Patiently, the doctor corrected the young resident and explained what would happen in my eye when the drops were put in.

My eye exam suggested several ideas about good supervision to me. I saw gentleness but firmness. I saw failure but recovery. I saw patience but persistence. I saw on-the-job learning undergirded by clear feedback.

My experience in that eye examination helped me define supervision.[6] To me, supervision is a supportive relationship which encourages growth through example, practice, and feedback.

Supervision by example calls on us to be willing to let others look over our shoulders. We put our own ministries on display under a microscope. The opportunity to see and question makes learning concrete.

Supervision through practice is learning by doing. It's hands-on experience, on-the-job training. What's second nature to the veteran in ministry has to be broken down into bite-sized hunks for the less experienced.

Supervision through feedback reminds us to affirm others first, then confront them about their areas of needed growth. We also must risk letting our supervisees fail, then critique results, and finally plan how to do better next time.

Ministry leaders have a supervisory role. But they practice supervision differently. Catalysts see supervision as a structured supportive relationship; followers know what to do and who will help them do their work. Commanders view supervision as an authoritarian situation, a boss-underling arrangement. Encouragers supervise by giving wide latitude and cheerleading the supervisee along. Hermits keep their distance, let people go their own way, and hope for responsible Self-Starters to carry the load.

Effective supervision involves a clearly structured, yet comfortable, relationship between a supervisor and a supervisee. The best supervisor I ever had was a man with whom I shared a ministry vision. We had a common task, and he delighted in making opportunities for me to move toward our goal. He didn't allow me to wander off target, but he opened every door he could for me that led toward our shared dream. He cared about me and the quality of my work. He gave me structure and support, both essentials in effective supervision.

Conflict: the Craft of Mediating

"Any leader can hold the helm when the sea is calm," announces the poster. Conflict tests any leader's mettle.

Conflict is threatening to most congregations. Most of us feel at least some discomfort with confrontation and disruption. But conflict within churches? Surely not! We're nice people, aren't we? Yes. But God cut out all of us with different cookie cutters. Our interpersonal mismatches in the church are taken personally like in any other group. So conflict occurs. Christians do have one advantage, however. We have pledged our allegiance to the Reconciler, the One whose life and death miraculously, but routinely, turns enemies into friends.

Why do Christians disagree? Other than basic human sinfulness, two additional sources of conflict are prevalent in congregations. First, we disagree over our differences. We differ over our goals, values, and personal backgrounds. Second, we disagree over our similarities. When there's only one of something in the church and more than one member wants that post or resource, you have conflict. For example, while I was a seminarian, my parents moved to another state and joined a new church. During my Christmas holiday school break, I worshiped with them in their new congregation. The worship bulletin contained an insert sheet asking for volunteer teachers and workers. I "volunteered" to serve as pastor of the church! If I had been at all serious about my "offer," the actual pastor and I would have been in conflict.

Most church conflicts center in differences over feelings, like personality clashes, or over facts, like a divisive event. Conflicts over feelings call for listening and ventilating. Conflicts over facts require good faith bargaining and negotiating. Effective leaders set the climate and shape the structure for both approaches to conflict management.

Catalysts take a partnership approach to conflict resolution. They know that problems are only solved and stay solved when the folks with the problems take steps to mediate their differences. The Catalyst acts to get the conflicting parties together and to get them involved in a conflict management process. But the final result depends on the competing parties.

Franklin Roosevelt had a favorite story about catalytic approaches to conflict management. It seems two Chinese coolies were arguing heatedly in the middle of a crowd. A stranger expressed surprise that, considering the intensity of the disagreement, no blows were being struck. Friends replied, "The man who strikes the first blow admits that his ideas have given out."

Commanders adopt a pusher stance toward conflict. They push people into ruffled feelings and polarization at times by their insistence on productivity. At other times, they push people toward settling their differences. Their forceful demands that others either shape up or ship out creates pressure. In other words, the Commander isn't very subtle in confronting conflict. He's a bit like the woman from Michigan who was awarded a divorce on the grounds that her husband had given each of their five children a saxophone. That is a little heavy-handed!

Encouragers work at pleasing people in conflict. They take a high stake in resolving interpersonal differences. They tend to rescue others rather than helping them solve their own problems. When someone comes to talk with an Encourager about some problematic monkey on his back, the odds are good that when the conversation is finished the Encourager will then have the monkey on his back. You can often spot Encouragers by the monkey collections they carry around on their backs.

Hermits run from conflict. They pull back and leave the pot of conflicts to boil unattended.

Applying Interactive Leadership

Craftsmanship is crucial for leaders. But how does interactive leadership work in a congregational setting? Three illustrations of this approach—team building, managing meetings, and providing leadership for the intangible aspects of congregational life—follow in the final three chapters of this book and demonstrate applications of interactive leadership.

Notes

1 Bruce Phillips, "Lost and Found," *Raleigh Times*, 1 Sept. 1983, p. 2C.

2 For a process for sharpening a congregation's vision, see Robert D. Dale, *To Dream Again* (Nashville: Broadman Press, 1981).

3 Ramona Jones, "Arlo Guthrie: On the Whole, He'd Rather Be In Poland," *Raleigh Times,* 21 Aug. 1981, p. 18.

4 James L. Esposito and Ralph L. Rosnow, "Corporate Rumors: How They Start and How to Stop Them," *Management Review,* Apr. 1983, pp. 44-49.

5 For useful materials on motivational climate, see Reginald M. McDonough, *Keys to Effective Motivation* (Nashville: Broadman Press, 1979); John Savage, *The Apathetic and Bored Church Member* (Pittsford: LEAD Consultants, 1976); Abraham Maslow, *Motivation and Personality,* 2nd ed. (New York: Harper and Row, 1970); and Frederick Herzberg, *The Motivation to Work* (New York: John Wiley and Sons, 1959).

6 Doran McCarty, *The Supervision of Ministry Students* (Atlanta: Home Mission Board, 1978).

III
Illustrating
an Interactive
Leader Style

7
The Art and Science
of Team Building

Teamwork pays dividends. If someone lends me a hand, together we can do things neither can do alone.

Shortly after World War II, Ed Sullivan invited Jimmy Durante to join him in a benefit show at a local veteran's hospital. Durante agreed. But he told Sullivan he had two radio broadcasts scheduled on that date and could only do one song for the wounded soldiers.

Durante sang to the disabled vets and got resounding applause. As a surprised Ed Sullivan watched from the wings, Jimmy Durante grabbed the microphone again and performed two complete routines. The soldiers gave Durante a standing ovation.

When Sullivan told Jimmy Durante he'd miss his radio shows now, Durante explained. "Look at those two guys in the center of the front row," he said. "Then you'll see why those radio shows became unimportant."

Peering between the curtains, Sullivan saw two one-armed soldiers seated together. They were applauding by clapping their remaining hands together. That's teamwork.

Most of us wish for a magic wand to make teams and committees more effective. We've heard the sad joke: "A camel is a horse put together by a committee." We know from experience that committees sometimes work slowly and poorly.

But leading work teams can become an exciting ministry opportunity if you become a team builder. One secret of effective church group leadership is team building.

Henry Ford described the importance of team building beautifully:

> Coming together is a beginning;
> keeping together is progress;
> thinking together is unity;
> working together is success.

God's people deserve the success working together brings. Are you willing to become an effective team builder?[1]

Team Building: Does My Church Need It?

Team building is needed in most churches. Can you recognize the need for team building in your congregation?

Positively, the need for team building revolves around one question: Do you have persons or groups who are required to work together? In other words, do you have committees, work teams, staff members, or councils with tasks assigned by the church? If so, you must become a team builder for them.

Negatively, several signs point to the need for greater team spirit.

- Meetings are boring, frustrating, and unproductive.
- There's little enthusiasm. Most folks appear to be just going through the motions.
- Work falls between the cracks and is left undone.
- I feel I'm the primary person working, and I don't think I can keep up this pace much longer.
- Everyone does his own thing and goes in his own direction.
- Communication is lousy. No one knows exactly what's going on.
- Organizations in our church don't seem to know or care what other church organizations are doing.
- Administratively, our left hand doesn't know what our right hand is doing. We aren't coordinated.

Now, does your church need team building? Are you ready to

guide the process of turning diverse interests and gifts toward central tasks?

Effective teams cooperate. Here's an example. A Boy Scout troop out for a hike discovered an abandoned section of railroad track. Each of them tried to walk the rails but eventually lost balance and stepped down.

Then two boys bet the others they could walk the entire length of track without falling off. Of course, the other scouts dared the two boys to make their brag good. The two stepped up on opposite rails and by holding hands for balance walked the entire distance without difficulty. Teams can be far more productive than competitors.

Team Building: What Is It?

Team building is turning diversity toward unity. That's my definition. Team building is needed anytime two or more persons depend on each other and work together: common goals; mutual respect; togetherness; interdependency; teamwork; high morale; support and encouragement. These are some key ingredients of team building.

From a theological perspective, the apostle Paul's body of Christ image (Rom. 12 and 1 Cor. 12) undergirds team building. See how Paul highlights both diversity and unity in the church: "For as in one body we have many members, and all the members do not have the same function, so we, though many, are one body in Christ, and individually members one of another" (Rom. 12:4-5).

Several leadership implications flow from Paul's description of Christ's body:

- The body of Christ is diverse, varied. Leadership and coordination are needed for effective ministry in congregations (Rom. 12:4-6).
- All of the body of Christ's natural diversity makes for richness. All varied parts are needed for the body to function well (1 Cor. 12:14-26).
- Christ provides unity for his body, the church (1 Cor.

12:12-13). Christ gives us a myriad of gifts to use in ministry. And he becomes the stack pole, the unifier, in the use of our ministry gifts.

Some wag has described an "ideal" church committee. With tongue in cheek, he claimed a committee is four persons with little time and interest and one person who likes to run things his own way anyway! That's not team building. Team building takes the stewardship of spiritual gifts seriously.

Team Building's Ten Commandments

Team building requires ambidextrous leaders.[2] That's because two issues must always be balanced in working teams: member needs and organizational mission. As leader, you're trying simultaneously to create a family atmosphere of concern and get a job done for the congregation at large. Your right hand—family atmosphere—must know what your left hand—the job—is doing and cooperate.

Here are ten principles to follow in team building. The first five spotlight people concerns and the second five focus on production issues. Remember they must be held in balanced tension. A team that deals with relationships alone becomes a party. On the other hand, a team preoccupied with their task only ignores members' hurts.

Both people and production are vital. In fact, in volunteer groups if the volunteers aren't fed spiritually and emotionally, they don't work. Napoleon once observed, "An army's effectiveness depends on its size, training, experience and morale . . . and morale is worth more than all the other factors combined."

● First Commandment: Develop personal ownership of your team's life and work. People support what they help create. Everyone wants a piece of the action. If I feel important individually to my group's progress, I contribute to its work. When I belong, I buy in and take ownership of my team's task.

● Second Commandment: Surface expectations. Everybody expects something from the groups they take part in. Family atmosphere is fostered when team members recognize there are differing personal agendas present within the team and can find enough common concerns to work together anyway.

● Third Commandment: Create a "we" climate. A family atmosphere depends on a sense of kinship, of feeling drawn together. Bear Bryant, the University of Alabama's late football coach claimed team building had three ingredients:

> If anything goes bad,
>> then I did it.
> If anything goes semigood,
>> then we did it.
> If anything goes real good,
>> then you did it.
> That's all it takes
>> to get people to win football games for you.

A "we" climate is encouraged when leaders take responsibility for failures and share the successes.

● Fourth Commandment: Recognize relational roles in teams. If a team takes care of its own members, a sense of family grows. A broad range of relational roles exists in any group. Note the sample checklist below. How do you provide leadership for team building's right hand? Mark your most characteristic response for each role option.

I'm a *harmonizer.* I'm a peacemaker who pours oil on troubled waters. I mediate differences and relieve tensions.

( ) Always   ( ) Sometimes   ( ) Never

I'm a *compromiser.* I meet other opinions halfway. I give ground and admit my mistakes when necessary.

( ) Always   ( ) Sometimes   ( ) Never

I'm a *gatekeeper.* I keep communication channels open. I facilitate others' participation.

( ) Always   ( ) Sometimes   ( ) Never

I'm a *standard setter.* I help set goals. I make my group measure its work by agreeing on standards.

( ) Always   ( ) Sometimes   ( ) Never

I'm a *commentator.* I keep track of my group's work. I interpret our internal progress to our own members.

( ) Always   ( ) Sometimes   ( ) Never

I'm a *follower.* I go along with the group's movement. I listen and let others express ideas.

( ) Always   ( ) Sometimes   ( ) Never

Analyze your orientation to your team's family atmosphere. If you checked a majority of "always" responses, you are obviously tuned in to relational needs in group settings. Whether you as a leader focus strongly on the relational roles in teamwork or not, people's needs must be attended to in volunteer groups. If you selected a majority of "never" responses, take steps to see that other team members help maintain the group's sensitivity of member's concerns.

● Fifth Commandment: Do team repair. Groups need maintenance and tune up work in order to run smoothly. Don't neglect family atmosphere.

Use the five principles listed above as guidelines for the relational side of team building. Now, let's consider some suggestions on the task dimension of leading teams.

● Sixth Commandment: Define the core mission of your organization. No team can function productively without a clear vision of its task. Just as important, a team needs to know how it can contribute to the overall mission of the larger organization. Help your congregation define its dream, and you'll increase the effectiveness of all the work teams in your church.

● Seventh Commandment: Identify the formal task groups you work with. A common problem church leaders face is the overlap of members' responsibilities. For example, a pastor may work with his staff, deacons, church council, finance committee, nominating committee, and a task force or two at any given period of time. Inevitably, the same faces show up on several work teams during the same church year. Just because work relationships are clearly defined on one team doesn't mean they will be on other teams even if (and especially if) the same people serve in several different church posts.

Identify each team you work with. List the members of each team. Note the overlapping members. Be aware of the different roles you're called on to provide in each setting. In other words, know when you change hats and select the right hat for each occasion.

● Eighth Commandment: Develop team task descriptions. Just as job descriptions cut down on gaps or overlaps in individual's work assignments, team task descriptions do too. Teams work more effectively when they are sure of their responsibilities.

● Ninth Commandment: Monitor task roles on your team. Several roles aid your team's work. Can you find yourself?

I'm an *initiator*. I propose solutions and changes. I suggest goals and procedures.

( ) Always   ( ) Sometimes   ( ) Never

I'm an *information seeker*. I ask for clarification of facts and options. I request additional facts.

( ) Always   ( ) Sometimes   ( ) Never

I'm an *opinion seeker*. I clarify values. I like to get group members' feelings out on the table.

( ) Always   ( ) Sometimes   ( ) Never

I'm an *information giver*. I share facts. I offer my pertinent experiences.

( ) Always   ( ) Sometimes   ( ) Never

I'm an *opinion giver*. I state my beliefs. I lobby for certain values.

( ) Always   ( ) Sometimes   ( ) Never

I'm an *elaborator*. I spell out possibilities and explore consequences. I lend supporting evidence.

( ) Always   ( ) Sometimes   ( ) Never

I'm a *coordinator*. I make connections between ideas. I enable group members to work together.

( ) Always   ( ) Sometimes   ( ) Never

I'm a *summarizer*. I define the progress our group has made and where we have departed from our original goals. I help keep our sense of direction clear.

( ) Always   ( ) Sometimes   ( ) Never

I'm an *evaluator.* I measure group progress by standards. I question practicality, logic, facts, or procedure.

( ) Always   ( ) Sometimes   ( ) Never

I'm an *energizer.* I push my group to act. I try to motivate toward "more" or "better."

( ) Always   ( ) Sometimes   ( ) Never

I'm an *assister.* I help my group by performing routine tasks. I distribute materials or do other things to help us get our work done.

( ) Always   ( ) Sometimes   ( ) Never

I'm a *recorder.* I, either formally or informally, make notes on group decisions. I keep the group's memory sharp.

( ) Always   ( ) Sometimes   ( ) Never

The roles above describe team building's left hand, the task orientation. Which roles do you as a leader use to get work accomplished? Note especially the total number of "always" and "never" responses.

Turn back to the fourth commandment and compare your relational approach to your task orientation. Which seems to predominate? What concrete steps can you take to be sure both a family atmosphere and the job to be done are balanced?

● Tenth Commandment: Learn to manage meetings. Guiding a process in meetings is better than controlling people. The next chapter of this book deals with meeting management.

Ambidextrous leaders make good team builders. Their right hands know what their left hands are doing as they balance relationships and tasks in work teams.

Team Building: a Model

Here's one model for team building. Picture a baseball diamond. Let each base designate an activity in team building for you. Like baseball, team building involves activities done repeatedly and in sequence.

First base is *sharing*. Effective teamwork depends on trust and understanding. Learning about each other enhances team building. A simple and natural way to heighten team spirit in church groups is to gather prayer concerns from team members and spend some group time in prayer.

A variety of sharing approaches helps team formation. In a men's retreat the church troublemaker opened up. He was an old man, a loner with a reputation for being negative and cantankerous. In a history-sharing session he told how he'd been abandoned as a child and raised by a Baptist pastor. "If that preacher hadn't taken me into his home," he said tearfully, "I don't know what would've become of me!"

The other men comforted him. The old man was surprised. "I didn't know you cared for me like this," he exclaimed. Interestingly, his pastor reports that incident was a turning point. Knowing he was a valued member of the group changed this old gentleman into a cooperative team contributor.

Second base is *affirming*. Another step in team building is taken when the demonstrated gifts of team members are affirmed. Encouragement is a necessary ingredient in esprit de corps.

She had served as church pianist during her high school years. Now she was resigning to go away to college. During her final worship service the minister placed a basket of cut flowers on the pulpit platform. Taking one, he presented it to the young pianist and thanked her for her specific contributions to the choirs and the worship climate. Then, he invited other members to take a flower and say a thank you. The flower supply was exhausted before all the thank you's were said. How the talented young pianist must have missed being part of that team!

Third base is *goal setting*. With individual understanding and group appreciation as a background, the assigned tasks of a group can be undertaken. Some leaders begin the game on third base. That is, they neglect the group-building relationships and move immediately to tasks. I've found some time spent in getting folks acquainted and committed to each other pays dividends in the quality and quantity of ministry produced later. Team members can agree on and take ownership of goals more readily when they know and value each other as persons and as Christians.

Home plate is *celebrating*. When persons care for each other and do good work together, completed tasks become an occasion for worship and celebration. Rejoicing over what God does is a natural reaction in religious communities.

Visualize the team-building model like this:

2.   Affirming

3.   Goal Setting   1.   Sharing

4.   Celebrating

Remember to run each base in turn. Keep running the bases too because one run wins few games. Keep on sharing, affirming, and goal setting each in turn. And there will be lots of occasions for celebrating.

Leaders' Perspectives on Team Building

Leaders bring their own perspectives to the team-building process. Catalysts refer to "our team." Commanders speak of "my staff." Encouragers think of terms as "my buddies." Hermits depict teamwork as "their concerns."

Cooperation is the bedrock ingredient of congregational team building. Edmund Hillary and his native guide Tenzing made history by climbing Mount Everest. On their descent, Hillary lost his footing and fell. Tenzing dug his ax into the ice and pulled Hillary back to safety. Later Tenzing refused to take any special credit for saving Sir Edmund Hillary's life. His view? "Mountain climbers always help each other." That's the attitude of team builders.

Team Building's Ultimate Goal

Any church is made up of a wide variety of teams. Some will work better than others. But the ultimate goal of team builders is to develop a congregational team. When all the diverse gifts, roles, and resources of a congregation are pooled for common causes, team building has been successful.

Paul saw diversity turned toward unity. He described team building's ultimate goal: "And his gifts were that some should be apostles, some prophets, some evangelists, some pastors and teachers, to equip the saints for the work of ministry, for building up the body of Christ, until we all attain to the unity of the faith and of the knowledge of the Son of God" (Eph. 4:11-13).

Notes

1 For an excellent general perspective on team building, see William G. Dyer, *Team Building: Issues and Alternatives* (Reading: Addison-Wesley, 1977).

2 For survey information on how to recognize and balance the process and content aspects of team building, see Walter M. Lifton, *Groups* (New York: John Wiley & Sons, 1972), pp. 1-28; David W. Johnson and Frank P. Johnson, *Joining Together* ((Englewood Cliffs: 1975), pp. 12-13.

8
Meetings, Meetings Everywhere: Can You Manage Them?

"Whoever invented the meeting must have had Hollywood in mind. I think they should consider giving Oscars for meetings: Best Meeting of the Year, Best Supporting Meeting, Best Meeting Based on Material from Another Meeting. . . . Meetings are everyone's salvation."[1] That's William Goldman's evaluation of how the movie industry functions.

"Salvation" overestimates the feeling of a majority of congregational meetings. According to most reports, in the church more meetings have a hellish flavor than a heavenly one. Interactive leaders can help make meetings more bearable and much more effective.

Meetings aren't always fun, but they are apparently necessary. For example, some experts estimate business managers spend one third to one half of their workweek in meetings. That may add up to 1,000 hours of meetings per year! Congregational leaders don't spend that much time in meetings. But because they work with volunteers, church leaders need to know what they're doing or their meetings won't be very comfortable or effective. What's more, they'll soon lose their followers. What are the issues at stake in successful meeting management?

When Is a Meeting Needed?

Meetings are generally settings for communicating with others and for building a consensus in groups. Not every occasion calls for a meeting, of course. Call a meeting when:

- Congregational issues need to be explored. The various members of the congregation can bring together bits of experience and facts that help define, analyze, and solve problems. This interplay of ideas, options, backgrounds, contradictions, and agreements can establish a creative base for dealing with community-wide issues.

- Opinions need to be surveyed and a consensus reached. Good decisions call for broad participation, widely shared information, and time for a natural consensus to emerge.

- Reports must be given verbally. Some reports can be written and circulated through the congregation. But when a report requires discussion, mutual understanding, and prompt action, then a meeting may be your best option.

- A team spirit is needed. Group roles are best defined in group settings. When the morale of members is at stake, meetings provide a setting in which teamwork can become the focus.

- Group goals are the basic agenda. Setting and selling goals are congregation-wide concerns which usually require meetings.

- Training members is necessary. Meetings provide settings for helping members know what to do as well as how to do it.

Don't Call Unnecessary Meetings

In one of British comedian John Cleese's films, he plays an overburdened executive. Hear his explanation to his wife about why he has to bring work home at night. "There's no time to work at work, darling. I have to go to meetings. If it wasn't for the sleep I get at meetings, I wouldn't be able to stay up and work."[2] It sounds like he's involved in some unnecessary meetings, doesn't it?

Meetings are only one structure for getting your point across or guiding the decision-making process. Don't overdo meetings. You probably shouldn't call a meeting when:

- Letters, memos, or phone calls will communicate the same information just as well.
- Needed participants can't attend.

- You don't have enough time to prepare to lead the meeting effectively.
- More time and effort are required of participants than the outcome justifies.

Planning for Meetings

Meetings require good planning. Before calling a meeting, answer a few questions.

What kind of meeting is it? What kind of resources are needed?

There are several types of meetings commonly used in congregational settings. Their purposes, primary uses, structures, and required leader skills are overviewed below.

Information Meetings

Purpose: Pass along basic facts needed to do work well.
Uses: (1) orientation and (2) teaching/training.
Formats: (1) mass forums, (2) panels, and (3) symposia.
Leader Skills:

- communication skills (speaking, writing, listening);
- ability to research and organize materials;
- development and use of visual aids (charts, graphs, newsprint, projected materials and media, chalkboard).

Problem-Solving Meetings

Purpose: Resolve difficult issues, untangle misunderstandings, and create new programs.
Uses:

- involving broad participation in problem research, definition, and resolution;
- pooling resources;
- hearing from experts, resource persons, and congregational legitimizers.

Formats: (1) brainstorming session and (2) staff reports to the larger group for their reflection and consensus.

Leader Skills:
- evenhandedness regarding viewpoints, options, and participation;
- defining and analyzing the actual problem;
- researching and fact finding;
- generating and exploring alternatives;
- summarizing and putting the facts into context;
- deciding on a solution and planning its implementation.

Procedural Meetings

Purpose: Develop a clear understanding of processes, principles, policies, and precedents.

Uses: (1) informing and (2) increasing psychological ownership.

Formats:
- open forum for making decisions and molding procedures;
- use the larger group to deal with staff recommendations on procedural matters;
- describe processes and ask participants to clarify and interpret them.

Leader Skills:
- flexibility—because policy meetings often switch back and forth between information and problem solving;
- clarifying group members' statements;
- gathering a broad audience;
- lecture ability.

What kind of agenda is required?

Orderliness helps any meeting. Before a meeting, tell participants what it's about, what's expected of them, when it will begin, how long it will last, when and where the meeting will be held, and who the other participants are. If decisions are to be made which will have congregational impact, be sure those who will be expected to implement the decisions are present. Also, involve key legitimizers and divergent views from the congregation.

When others are involved in the agenda too, provide a rehearsal for them. Their anxiety will be lessened, and the smoothness and effectiveness of the meeting will be improved.

A draft copy of the agenda is often circulated so that participants can add items of personal concern. Posting the agenda on newsprint or on a chalkboard allows a quick review and any needed expansion at the beginning of a work session. You may also want to ask your group to prioritize the agenda items to give you an indication of their areas of energy and the amount of time to be allotted to the various items.

Will materials need to be prepared in advance?

Copies of the agenda, pertinent documents, and working papers may be needed for premeeting study or for distribution during the session itself. Make these items attractive and easy to use with punched paper, color-coded work sheets, and tabbed folders as desired.

Who and how many will attend?

This isn't just a question of sufficient room and enough chairs. There are two more important questions: (1) Do these participants know each other?, and (2) How will I subdivide them into smaller groups, if needed?

First, are the group members acquainted? Work groups come in three varieties: family, cousin, and stranger groups. Family groups enjoy close relationships and longer histories together. Some church groups, especially in small, stable, and heterogeneous congregations, may be family groups. Cousin groups have some history together but fairly casual relationships. Probably the majority of congregational work groups are cousin groups. The stranger group has little or no previous history and only situational or accidental relationships.

Cousin groups are deceiving. They appear to know each other but really don't. They appear cooperative but may really be competitive. They appear loyal to the larger congregation but may have individual interests or subgroup alliances that erode their ties to the church's vision.

Second, how can large groups be structured into manageable smaller work units? The size of small groups depends on your goals and your resources. Here are some general guidelines for structuring small groups.

Use groups of six to twelve when your goals are low-key discussion, general sharing, optional participation, or care for the members of the subgroup. The special resources you'll need are at least one get-acquainted session before any difficult tasks are assigned, trained group leaders, an informal setting, and seventy-five minutes of session time.

Use groups of four when you intend to have everyone participate and accept responsibility. You'll need flexible space, skilled platform leadership, and at least forty-five minutes of work time. These groups form quickly and require no internal group leader if the general leader can give clear instructions from the platform.

Use groups of three when your goals and resources are the same as groups of four but you only have thirty minutes in your schedule.

Use groups of two when your goals are confrontation or in-depth sharing. You'll need participants who are comfortable sharing, a setting where informal conversation in pairs is natural, people who either know each other in advance or are willing to risk relating, members with listening skills, and a minimum of thirty minutes of work time.

One Method for Guiding Meetings

Most leaders prefer a set routine for guiding meetings.[4] I use a "ministry cycle" to give me a framework for leading meetings. Why? First, this four-step approach provides me a mental picture of the processes in guiding a meeting from convening it to acting finally on its decisions. Second, with a model in mind, I can control the process, not the people. If I remain closely focused on the congregation's basic mission and the meeting management model, I'm less apt to fall into manipulation.

Evaluating, creating, deciding, and ministering are the ongoing processes to be managed in meetings. Note that "-ing" endings are used to show these processes are ongoing. Here's how the model unfolds.

Step One—Evaluating

Begin a meeting by demonstrating to your work group exactly where your mutual task stands. Evaluating, in this sense, can be accomplished in a number of ways.

● Identify the overall mission of the congregation, or more likely, the slice of the mission your group has been assigned by the larger congregation.

● Describe your group's specific task and mandate for acting.

● Recount the history of events which has brought your group to this point in its work.

● Review the status of your group's work to date by measuring your progress against the congregation's purpose.

Step Two—Creating

Developing a range of alternatives is the next step in the ministry cycle model. Several activities can be used in the search for problem-solving possibilities.

● Plan to identify three or four options for coping with your group's task. These possibilities may provide a broad enough and rich enough set of alternatives to combine or reshape them into some distinctively different final solution. Besides, additional options can give you a "Plan B" to fall back on if your preferred solution fails.

● Set a mood of playfulness. Relaxed attitudes and atmospheres let thinkers manipulate ideas more easily. E. B. White wrote in humorist James Thurber's obituary, "During his happiest years, Thurber did not write the way a surgeon operates (as Thurber had described his writing approach), he wrote the way a child skips rope, the way a mouse waltzes." Help your group members play with ideas, and they'll be more likely to develop creative options.

● Allow enough time for the process of creativity to take root. Edison claimed his inventions were the result of 1 percent inspiration and 99 percent perspiration. Give unconscious minds a chance to work. Here's what happened when engine designer Franz Hauk proposed a five-cylinder engine for the Audi 5000. First, Hauk's bosses smiled. Then, they gave him time and freedom to create. At Audi they have a saying, "When a man has a big idea, we put him in a room and leave him alone." The Audi brass left Hauk alone for three and a half years! The result? He developed a revolutionary new engine.[5]

● Brainstorm possibilities. Encourage your group to envision lots of solutions without critiquing any of the ideas initially. A number of variations on brainstorming are available. For example, recently I asked a group of twenty ministers how they would provide a full church program if gasoline became so scarce their members could only make one trip each week to the church building. Their general reaction was dumbfoundedness. Then, using a method of structured brainstorming, we generated over fifty solutions in ten minutes. In another twenty minutes we had designed five major strategies and fairly detailed plans to pursue each option.[6] All of these possibilities came from a group who originally thought they were stymied.

● Take your group's ideas from brainstorming or from other sources and stretch them by applying the "scamper" acronym.[7] Here's an overview of this method for expanding old ideas and generating new ones.

- S—What can you substitute?
- C—What can you combine?
- A—What can you adapt?
- M—What can you magnify, miniaturize, and multiply?
- P—What can you put to other uses?
- E—What else? How else? Where else?
- R—Can you rearrange or reverse?

Step Three—Deciding

When a full range of options is available to your group, the difficult but exciting process of selecting the most promising solution becomes the agenda. Consider these principles of decision making in an interactive setting.[8] These approaches may be applied to a committee or in the congregation at large.

• Involve all of the implementers of the decision in making the initial decision.

• Create a decision-making forum. Review the history of the decision you're facing, the other options which have been considered, and the facts, opinions, and experiences which have yielded the option(s) you're presenting for the group's explorations.

• When possible, make group decisions by consensus. This style of decision making takes longer. But consensus builds more psychological ownership for implementation because people are heard and valued, and they hear and learn from others' ideas. Additionally, time pressure to "decide now" is lessened, and better decisions are apt to emerge. The usual temptation is to vote, count the majority, and go home. But voting divides. Fifty one percent may carry the decision, but in voluntary organizations fifty one percent of the members is rarely enough to implement that decision.

• Become aware of how your group's members act in decision-making settings. Various types of participants can aid the decision-making process. The participants who adopt active behaviors in groups, however, provide the most momentum for creative decision making and effective ministry.

Step Four—Implementing

At this point, planning, delegating, and executing your group's decision take center stage. Active ministry outside of the meeting now becomes the congregation's prime focus. These actions provide the grist for a new ministry cycle and a new series of later meetings as they may become necessary.

Leading the Ministry Cycle Approach

Observe that three principles allow a leader to guide meetings using the ministry cycle approach. As we'll see later, different leader styles set distinctive tones for the meetings themselves.

● The leader keeps the group's energy focused on one activity of the ministry cycle at a time. This keeps the group centered on the content level of their work.

● The leader maintains the momentum of the group by closely observing the sequence of the ministry cycle. This focuses on the process aspect of group life.

● The leader sums up the group's progress and triggers the movement of the group to the next ministry cycle activity. This refocusing sharply increases the group's energy. The triggering process is uniquely the leader's perogative.

Leader Styles and Meeting Management

Each of our four congregational leader styles can be used in guiding meetings. Each style flavors the meeting distinctively.

The Catalyst *participates freely* in all four ministry cycle steps. He contributes his ideas and resources but uses his influence primarily in summing up, triggering movement to the next step, and refocusing the group's energy on the appropriate aspect of the process. The Catalyst utilizes all the gifts of all of the group members in his management of the ministry cycle.

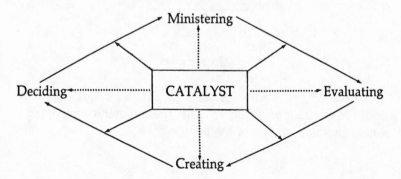

The Commander *runs* meetings by also taking an active role. However, he lobbies for his ideas as well as clearly guiding the meeting process.

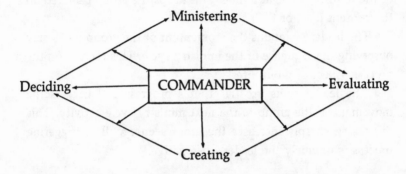

The Encourager *hosts* meetings and contributes his ideas a bit more selectively. He focuses enough on interpersonal issues in the group that he doesn't keep the meeting process sharply defined or moving crisply.

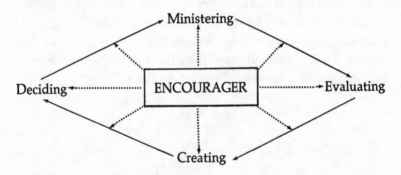

The Hermit *feels on-the-spot* in meetings. His discomfort keeps him from contributing positively to either the communicating or consensus-building aspects of the session.

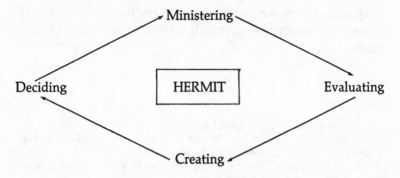

So You're Chairperson

Congregational leaders are sometimes faced with chairing a formal decision-making conference requiring careful observance of parliamentary law. A meeting model isn't all you'll need then. But don't be intimidated. Follow these fundamental principles.[9]

- Discuss only one subject at a time.
- Assure each member equal rights to speak, offer motions, hold office, and vote.
- Provide full and free debate.
- Protect majority and minority rights.
- Hold up the ideal of teamwork for the sake of the organization's health and effectiveness.

As a chairman, you're responsible for:

- keeping the meeting moving;
- knowing Robert's *Rules of Order* and your congregation's constitution and bylaws well enough to keep the meeting orderly;
- maintaining fairness;
- preserving harmony.

Would You Attend?

Meetings, meetings everywhere—and you can master the management of these eternal events. Plan, use the model for the actual meeting, apply parliamentary rules, and you'll find meetings more productive. Remember—never call a meeting you wouldn't attend yourself.

Notes

1 "Touring Cloud-Cuckoo-Land," *Time,* 4 Apr. 1983, p. 74.

2 "Monty Python's John Cleese Pursues a Not-so-silly Walk of Life—Making Business-Training Films," *People,* 26 Sept. 1983, p. 84.

3 Ralph E. Osborne, "Twelves? Fours? Twos?—The Why and How of Small Groups," *Open Circle,* June 1974, pp. 1-2.

4 For some helpful suggestions on guiding meetings, Brian O'Connell, *Effective Leadership in Voluntary Organizations,* (Chicago: Follett Publishing, 1976), pp. 82-94.

5 "When I Proposed a 5-Cylinder Engine for the Audi 5000, They Smiled," *Time,* 14 Nov. 1977, p. 9

6 Charles H. Clark, *Idea Management: How to Motivate Creativity and Innovation,* (New York: AMACOM, 1980), p. 35-45.

7 Ibid., p. 16.

8 Luke T. Johnson, *Decision Making in the Church: A Biblical Model,* (Philadelphia: Fortress Press, 1983).

9 Edmund Haugen, *Mister, Madam Chairman* (Minneapolis: Augsburg Publishing, 1963).

9
Leading the Intangible Congregation

Walter Lippmann, the American journalist, once described America under fire as caught between unloving critics and uncritical lovers. Sometimes churches get squeezed in the same vise. Congregations need interactive leaders who love them critically to keep them from petrifying, to help them face their imperfections, and to encourage growth with integrity. Critical love requires leadership for intangible factors of congregational life.

Leadership and Informal Organization

Traditionally, pastoral management and church administration courses have taught us to lead the formal, goal-oriented side to the congregation. At times we've assumed that the formal, "organizational chart" aspect of congregations is all there is to lead.

Experience teaches us to recognize another element of congregational life. The informal organization, the subterranean aspect of the congregation which emerges spontaneously to meet members' needs, must be led too.[1] I discovered the informal organizational phenomenon while pastoring a mission church. At intervals I would suggest some program to the congregation. They'd discuss it briefly, vote to adopt the program, then never lift a finger to make it a reality. After this action became an observed pattern, I felt a lot of frustration and confusion. Then I did some detective work. I discovered a church fuss had occurred shortly before I moved into that pastorate. The conflict had been so painful that the congregation had "agreed" not to disagree again. When a potentially disruptive issue faced them, they would no longer debate it. Instead, they would vote yes with their hands and no with their feet. Consequently, we had a number of unsupported programs and some policies no one followed. Formally, we set goals. Then, the informal organization took over and negated those official goals. I learned several lessons from these incidents, primarily that the informal organization is often more powerful than the formal one.

Leaders can take steps to minister through the informal organization.

● Keep the congregation involved in goal setting. Broad participation helps bring the informal, human need to have control over your own life into line with the formal tasks of the congregation.

● Demonstrate to members that they are cared for. Interpersonal needs will be met one way or the other. Making the care of members a mainstream goal of the congregation weds the formal and informal concerns of the organization.

Both the formal and informal organizations need leadership. The formal organization is the Commander's forte because of his emphasis on goals and production. The informal organization's response to the emerging needs of members matches the Encourager's comfort with relational ministries. The Catalyst identifies and tries to work with both the formal and informal organizations of his congregation. Unfortunately, the Hermit connects with neither dimension of organization.

Leadership and Institutional Climate

If leadership sets the pace in a congregation, climate sets the tone. Every congregation has an atmosphere, a spirit. It may be warm or cold, confident or fearful, reaching out or ingrown, generous or stingy. Revealed in its climate is a congregation's basic values, its "social glue."[2]

Climate is so important that management theorists describe it as the corporation's "religion."[3] For instance, IBM emphasizes three shared beliefs: (1) all employees should be treated with dignity and respect; (2) the company should accomplish every task with excellence; and (3) the customer should be given the best possible service. These beliefs demonstrate a view of human beings and a quest for excellence that smacks of a corporate faith. IBM's management team attributes the company's success over the past thirty years to its corporate culture.[4] No wonder climate is described, along with personal motives and needs, as the "second blade of the motivational scissor."[5]

All congregations develop a cultural climate. That is, congregations define "some interrelated set of beliefs, shared by most of their members, about how people should behave at work and what tasks and goals are important."[6] Climate exerts a powerful influence on the way members view their work and lives. Remember the story from medieval times about the traveler who met three stonecutters along a road and asked what each was doing. "I'm cutting stone," the first replied. "I'm shaping a cornerstone," said the second. But the third answered, "I am building a cathedral." Congregations with healthy climates are trying to develop cathedral builders, not mere stonecutters.

In the final analysis, your congregation's climate determines how it feels to serve through and be served by your church.[7] The key? Trust! Trust is the fundamental ingredient in the climate of a volunteer organization. However, other supporting elements help establish and maintain the congregation's culture too.

- Identity—Members enjoy belonging and feeling valued.
- Warmth—Fellowship is good; members feel well liked.
- Support—Leaders are helpful; mutual assistance is available.
- Responsibility—Members feel a measure of freedom to do their own job and fill their own niche.
- Challenge—Members know what the acceptable levels of risk taking are but feel stretched.
- Reward—Members receive emotional and spiritual "payment" and feel satisfaction and recognition for work that's well done.

- Standards—Members share the congregation's commitment to quality.
- Conflict—Members know inevitable differences will be dealt with openly; different opinions will be fairly heard.
- Structure—Members recognize that procedures, channels, and rules are clearly defined and broadly accepted.

Leaders are the primary congregational climate molders. Look at this classic case from the business world of the leader's impact on corporate culture.

> S. C. Allyn, a retired chairman of the board, likes to tell a story about his company—the National Cash Register Corporation. It was August 1945, and Allyn was among the first allied civilians to enter Germany at the end of the war. He had gone to find out what had happened to an NCR factory built just before the war but promptly confiscated by the German military command and put to work on the war effort. He arrived via military plane and traveled through burned-out buildings, rubble, and utter desolation until he reached what was left of the factory. Picking his way through bricks, cement, and old timbers, Allyn came upon two NCR employees whom he hadn't seen for six years. Their clothes were torn and their faces were grimy and blackened by smoke, but they were busy clearing out the rubble. As he came closer, one of the men looked up and said, "We knew you'd come!" Allyn joined them in their work and together the three men began cleaning out the debris and rebuilding the factory from the devastation of war. The company had even survived the ravages of a world war.
>
> A few days later, as the clearing continued, Allyn and his coworkers were startled as an American tank rumbled up to the site. A grinning GI was at its helm. "Hi," he said, "I'm NCR, Omaha. Did you guys make your quota this month?" Allyn and the GI embraced each other. The war may have devastated everything around them, but NCR's hard driving, sales-oriented culture was still intact.[8]

It's clear that climate lives through thick and thin. It's just as obvious that organizational spirit molds behavior.

How can leaders exert a crucial influence on their congregations? Is there a strategy for building a good climate? While there's no magic formula for impacting a congregation's climate, several broad actions make a difference.[9]

● Vision and values are articulated by the leader. Leaders leave their mark through creating a guiding dream and by shaping shared beliefs.

● Positive reinforcement is offered by the leader. One large corporation has developed a playful ritual with a serious meaning. They present a plaque to productive employees called the "Attaboy." A ceremony accompanies the "Attaboy's" award. While it's all done in high good humor, the recipients know they've been recognized for a significant accomplishment in the company. The award apparently boosts morale throughout this corporation's work force.

● Communication of the climate's major values by the leader offers extra leverage. Sermons, study sessions, and special events provide opportunities to define, preserve, or change the congregation's climate.

● Developing human resources is a key occasion for climate building. Enlisting and training workers as well as recruiting and assimilating new members lend settings in which the values the congregation takes seriously can be communicated.

● The enhancement of organizational and physical resources also sets the stage for molding the congregation's culture. Designing the ministry structure, developing the administrative policies, "paying volunteers," and even decorating the work environment all suggest important clues to the church's climate.

Congregational climates[10] are the outgrowth of leader's styles and follower's motivations. Note the four patterns below and how they reflect the congregational leadership model.

● *Health-motivated climates* are usually the result of Catalyst's leadership. This climate emphasizes members' responsibility, encourages innovation, rewards excellence, and values teamwork.

● *Power-motivated climates* generally grow out of the Commander's style. This climate emphasizes production, provides structured rules, uses formal authority, and values loyalty.

● *Relationship-motivated climates* tend to develop from the Encourager's style. This climate emphasizes warm friendships, reinforces mutual support, provides freedom, and values acceptance.

● *Security-motivated climates* ordinarily emerge out of the Hermit's style. This climate emphasizes personal safety, discourages risk, reduces threats, and values protection.

Climate is set early in a congregation's life. Therefore, climate is more easily shaped in younger, smaller congregations. Setting the tone in older, larger, more diverse memberships is trickier. For instance, businesses have discovered that by the third generation of management the organizational climate has lost its clear focus.[11] Reshaping the congregational climate, then, becomes a major challenge for leaders of mature, complex, and pluralistic organizations.

Leadership and Organizational Stages

Congregations move through a range of organizational stages during their life spans. Each phase of institutional development calls for tailor-made leadership responses. Three biblical examples illustrate different stages and the varied demands leaders face at each phase.

Leaders for Organizational Beginnings

The start-up phase of any enterprise demands visionary generalists. Their vision gives purpose and direction to largely undefined organizations. Generalist skills are important to new groups since the demands are broad, and the participants are often few or unseasoned. New organizations are required to focus their limited resources on only the projects essential to their effectiveness.

Moses is an illustration of a biblical leader who functioned at a beginning point. He joined with God in the project of nation making. Moses helped deliver Israel from Egypt and led in establishing the nation in a Promised Land.

Moses apparently adopted primarily a Commander-styled leader role and found a dependent people ready to lean heavily on his strong personality. But the responsibilities of national leadership became so heavy, Moses had to change his leader style to a Catalyst approach—with the help of an external consultant, his father-in-law Jethro.

A number of vital reminders related to institutional start-up grow out of this incident in Moses' life.

• Trying to lead every facet of a group's life will cost leaders dearly both as persons and as family guides. Jethro returned Moses' wife and two sons to him. Apparently, nation making had become so heavy that Moses had "sent her away" (Ex. 18:2) and had given up his family responsibilities. He had committed what industrial psychologists describe as "corporate bigamy," being wed to both job and family.

• An objective outsider can often help leaders assess their work from a fresh perspective (Ex. 18:13-18).

• Delegation allows top leadership to concentrate on essentials and creates opportunities for other leaders to grow and contribute their skills to unformed enterprises (Ex. 18:19-27). Delegation permits a leader to "manage by exception," allowing policy and precedent to guide except in unusual situations requiring the leader's intervention.

• Select the best people available for leadership teams. Jethro suggested choosing "able men from all the people, such as fear God, men who are trustworthy and who hate a bribe" (Ex. 18:21). Good leaders realize that personnel decisions either help or haunt them for a long time. Selecting fellow leaders can't be allowed to deteriorate into politics. No organization outgrows its leadership.

• A leader in ministry always has a pastoral responsibility (Ex. 18:19). I was reminded of the pastoral dimension of my work after I'd led a management seminar for Virginia pastors. The content of the conference had gotten technical at some points. A participant, an old seminary friend, thanked me for my work and then added,

"But I don't work for IBM." I was grateful for his candor. Ministry leaders can't forget the personal aspect of their work.

• The result of effective delegation yields less pressure on top leaders. Additionally, a climate of harmony grows out of the sharing of responsibility (Ex. 18:23).

• Moses belatedly discovered an important leadership principle: people support what they help create. This insight is especially critical for leaders of new ventures with limited resources.

Leaders for Transitions

History is on the move, although its progress is virtually imperceptible at times. Nothing holds still for us very long. Therefore, some significant organizational changes unfold without great trauma. These transitions are often guided by gifted but fairly unspectacular leaders.

Nehemiah provided catalytic leadership for Israel during a turning point in her history. Under Persian domination, the city of Jerusalem and the worship patterns of the Jews fell into disrepair. Nehemiah, with a divine mandate as well as political assistance from Persian King Artaxerxes, returned to Jerusalem, guided the rebuilding of the walls of Jerusalem, and renewed public worship. This devout layman ministered through city management. Nehemiah reminds church people of how vital the leadership of laypersons is to the overall health and mission of the kingdom of God.

Numerous lessons grow out of Nehemiah's ministry during transition.

• Organizational diagnosis calls for listening and getting adequate and accurate facts (Neh. 1:1-3).

• Prayer can be used by religious leaders to increase insight into challenges (Neh. 1:4-11). Prayer and self-discovery go together. But Nehemiah didn't demand or expect instant insight. It's obvious from the frequency of Nehemiah's recorded prayers that he habitually depended on his relationship with God (Neh. 1:4-6; 2:4; 4:4,9; 5:19; 6:14; 13:14,22,29).

• Use the resources you have. As winetaster and server to

the king, Nehemiah had the possibility of using all of the king's resources, and he did (Neh. 2:1-4).

• There is power in a solid plan. Nehemiah had an idea and devised a plan to implement his idea (Neh. 2:5-8). Nehemiah realized that ultimately there are no unspiritual resources for God's purposes. God can use any resource—even a Persian king—to bring his intentions into reality.

• Timing is crucial—even in gradual transitions. Nehemiah kept his mission to himself for three days. His sense of good timing accomplished two ends: there was no advance warning for enemies, and it took advantage of the biblical concept of *kairos,* the opportune moment (Neh. 2:11-18).

• Team effort makes formidable tasks easier. Nehemiah was an effective team builder. Good morale and healthy group climate advance significant jobs (Neh. 3; 4:15-23).

• Delegating crucial tasks shares the burdens of top leadership while strengthening other leaders for the future (Neh. 7: 1-4).

• Worship celebrations mark important new beginnings and symbolize commitments (Neh. 8—13).

Leaders for Growth Booms

Occasionally the favorable factors in a situation flow together and a period of marked growth results. Effective leaders for growth eras are often single-minded persons with an uncanny ability to understand and bridge the old and the new. Barnabas was such a leader.

Barnabas was the first Christian in the biblical record to bridge the gap between the Greek and Jewish world. Since he had been born a Cypriot and raised a Levite, Barnabas in his own life linked the Hellenistic world and the Jewish-Christian religious communities. He used his blended background well in becoming a church stabilizer and a missionary.

Several features of Barnabas's leader style suggest these approaches for growth situations.

● Trustworthiness makes leaders followable. When the Jerusalem church needed a helper to stabilize the new church in Antioch, they sent Barnabas (Acts 11:22-26). Barnabas didn't assume a superior, "religious inspector" role. Barnabas knew that trust grows out of good experiences. That is, we prove ourselves trustworthy by our actions. Barnabas served well and was apparently able to present himself to the new Christians at Antioch in a nonthreatening way.

● Encouraging others and building them up is a basic leadership task. Barnabas was nicknamed the "Son of encouragement" (Acts 4:36). His encouragement showed itself in friendships and generosity. Barnabas sponsored Paul in Jerusalem (Acts 9:27) and later at Antioch (Acts 11:22-26). Barnabas's first appearance in the Acts record shows him as a generous steward of his resources (Acts 4:32-37).

● Balancing the task and relationship dimensions of ministry is vital. Barnabas was not only an encourager, he was a missionary who could get the job done too (Acts 11:23-24; 13:2 *ff.*). Concern for persons and commitment to production are fundamental ingredients in effective organizational leadership. Some growth-oriented Commanders take a "bigger-at-any-price" attitude which values numbers above fellowship. They see their organization become larger while the morale of their group diminishes.

● Managing conflict constructively is a basic skill for leaders of growing organizations. Barnabas and Paul disagreed sharply over whether or not to take another chance on John Mark who had dropped out in the middle of their first missionary journey. Their disagreement was so strong that they split up as a missionary team. But rather than criticize each other or take other steps that might undermine the missionary enterprise, they simply organized two missionary teams and continued their effective work separately (Acts 15: 36-41).

● Selecting people who can get the job done is an essential leadership opportunity. When Barnabas had done all for the Antioch church that he knew to do, he recruited Paul to help them

(Acts 11:25-26). Leaders need an eye for talent.

● Training others to a level so they can replace the original trainer secures the future of organizations. Barnabas helped both Paul and John Mark outgrow him. Their development was good for the kingdom of God. Apparently Barnabas was secure enough that he counted their personal growth a blessing, not a threat.

● Leaders must learn to follow too. Barnabas was Paul's mentor, but Paul became the more famous leader rather quickly. As far as the biblical record shows, Barnabas never fretted about being displaced in the top slot. That's a good attitude for leaders. Unless you're an absolute dictator or an oriental potentate, you'll sometimes be a leader and at other times a follower.

Intangibility and Leadership

The intangible congregation pleads for leadership too. Its informal organization, its climate, and the various stages of institutional life are real and require skilled responses from both leaders and the whole congregation.

Notes

1 For information on the informal organization, see Robert D. Dale, *To Dream Again* (Nashville: Broadman, 1981), pp. 80-85; and O. Jeff Harris, Jr., *Managing People at Work* (New York: John Wiley and Sons, 1976), pp. 111-132.

2 Edwin L. Baker, "Managing Organizational Culture," *Management Review*, July 1980 p. 8. For additional perspective on organizational climates, see Robert F. Allen and Charlotte Kraft, *The Organizational Unconscious* (New York: Spectrum, 1982).

3 Ibid.

4 Ibid.

5 Marlene Wilson, *The Effective Management of Volunteer Programs* (Boulder: Volunteer Management Associates, 1976), p.57.

6 Baker, "Managing Organizational Culture," p.8.

7 Wilson, *The Effective Management of Volunteer Programs*, pp. 58-59.

8 Terrence E. Deal and Allan A. Kennedy, *Corporate Cultures* (Reading: Addison-Wesley, 1982), pp. 3-4.

9 Baker, "Managing Organizational Culture," pp. 11-13.

10 See Wilson, *The Effective Management of Volunteer Programs*, pp. 59-60.

11 Edgar H. Schein, "The Role of the Founder in Creating Organizational Culture," *Organizational Dynamics*, Summer 1983, 13-28.

Leaders ma___ ___ ___ __ __ create ____ ideas ___ ___ ___tu-
tions. Eventua___ __ ___ ___erally ___ ___ ___ ___ ___rint.

One leader ____ ___ally invented the ___ ___ ___ ___as the
first teacher o___ ___ ___ ___ ___ ___ ___ ___merican
newspaper edi___. ___ ___ ___ ___ ___dation for
American educa___ ___ ___ ___acked Spell-
er" that sold n___ ___ ___is lifetime. He
created a comm___

Noah Webste___ ___ ___ive years, produced
his 70,000-word ___ ___ ___ary may be America's
most valuable s___ ___ ___ork gave us a common
language and, th___ ___ ___uring Noah Webster's lifetime, Italy had so___ ___ Italians couldn't talk to each
other. Webster sa___ ___ ___ that fate. He standardized our
language and ma___ ___ ___n. He invented America.

Noah Webster ___ ___ maker, a leader. He met needs. He
had a vision. The r___ ___ __ of his leadership, consequently, still
laps up on the sho___ ___ American's ideas and institutions.

Let congregation___ leaders create ripples too. Let these ripples
build healthier, stronger churches and grow more mature believers
in Christ.